THE ENTREPRENEURSHIP SERIES

· ·

Entrepreneurship and How to Establish
Your Own Business

SECOND EDITION

· ·

D1737970

Other books in The Entrepreneurship Series:

Human Resource Management

Basic Principles of Financial Management for a Small Business

Marketing for a Small Business

Management of a Small Business

Computing for a Small Business

Entrepreneurial Skills

The Franchise Option – How to Franchise Your Business

Forthcoming titles in this series:

Import, Export and Internationalisation of a Business

Strategic Management of a Small Business

About the authors ...

Cecile Nieuwenhuizen (Chapters 1 and 6) is a deputy chief lecturer in the Department of Business Management at Technikon SA. She holds the degrees BA (Comm), MBL and PhD (Criteria for the Financing of Small Industries) and a diploma in Small Business Management. She has co-authored books on strategic management and entrepreneurship, presented papers at international conferences and been involved in various small and medium enterprises as director and consultant.

Elbeth le Roux (Chapters 4 and 5) was the Executive Director of the Programme Group Business Management and Vice Principal at Technikon SA. She holds the degrees BCom and BCom (Hons) and MCom. She has co-authored and edited other books on management. She is now retired.

Hannelize Jacobs (Chapters 2 and 3) is a senior lecturer in the Department of Business Management at the Rand Afrikaans University. She holds the degrees BCom (Ed), BCom (Hons) and MCom. She has co-authored several books and specifically wrote on entrepreneurship.

THE ENTREPRENEURSHIP SERIES

Entrepreneurship and How to Establish Your Own Business

SECOND EDITION

C Nieuwenhuizen

EE Le Roux

H Jacobs

Consulting Editor: JW Strydom

Series Co-ordinating Editor: Cecile Nieuwenhuizen

JUTA

In appreciation of the entrepreneurial spirit of all the people who shared their knowledge and experience, gave inputs and contributed to this book for the benefit of developing entrepreneurs.

Entrepreneurship and How to Establish Your Own Business

First published 1996

Second impression 1997

Third impression 1997

Second edition 2001

Second impression 2003

Third impression 2003

Fourth impression 2004

ISBN 0 7021 5542 X

© Juta & Co. Ltd

PO Box 24309, Lansdowne 7779

Didactic Advisor: CCDD

Editor (second edition): Alfred LeMaitre

Book design and typesetting: Charlene Bate

Illustrations: Mark Bates, André Plant

Cover design: Inspiration Sandwich

Icons: Carol Nelson

Printed in South Africa by Mills Litho, Cape Town

CONTENTS

. . . .

CHAPTER 1: ENTREPRENEURSHIP AND SMALL BUSINESS MANAGEMENT IN PERSPECTIVE

. . . .

CHAPTER 2: BASIC BUSINESS CONCEPTS FOR THE PROSPECTIVE ENTREPRENEUR

· ·

CHAPTER 3: THE IDENTIFICATION OF FEASIBLE SMALL BUSINESS IDEAS

. . . .

CHAPTER 6: SETTING UP A BUSINESS

PREFACE

Often we know that we can and will start a business but realize that we need guidance. In this book we aim to guide people who have the will and desire to start and manage their own businesses successfully. Entrepreneurship often comes naturally, and the entrepreneur knows instinctively how to start a business. However it is beneficial to learn from other successful entrepreneurs to avoid making unnecessary mistakes which can be demotivating.

In the development phase of the book, people who started and managed their own businesses were consulted. They gave valuable inputs as to the information they needed in the different phases of start-up. These needs are addressed in a practical, informative way in this guide to establishing your own business.

The contributors to the book combined their personal experience in small business management with interviews, consultation and research done in the field of entrepreneurship and small business management.

The result is a practical guide to analyse yourself and your abilities critically, to evaluate business ideas with an open mind and to plan your business proactively. We aim to teach you how to:

- be positive about and use even your seemingly most insignificant talents, skills and knowledge, but to acknowledge your weak points and do something about them;
- be creative yet practical in your search for business ideas and believe in whatever you attempt;
- research your business idea and ensure that it will be profitable;
- plan the way you will be doing business and handle important issues like financing the start-up and marketing your product or service.

The willingness to learn is the first step in realising your dream to start your own business. If you have the desire to be successful it is possible to achieve success. We hope this book, the first in a range of eleven books on small business management, will make you enthusiastic about learning more and doing better.

Remember, by learning, looking and doing you can achieve success. Have fun in planning and starting your own business and good luck.

Cecile Nieuwenhuizen
2002

KEY TO ICONS

Four icons are used throughout this text to depict different components of the interactive learning process:

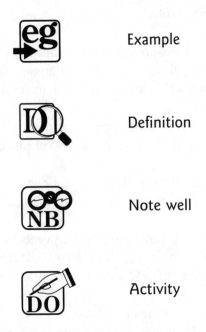

Example

Definition

Note well

Activity

ENTREPRENEURSHIP AND SMALL BUSINESS MANAGEMENT IN PERSPECTIVE

1 LEARNING OBJECTIVES (OUTCOMES)

After you have studied this chapter, you should be able to:

❏ define the term 'entrepreneur';
❏ indicate the similarities and differences between entrepreneurship, a small business enterprise and small business management;
❏ know which key factors contribute to successful entrepreneurship;
❏ give a critical evaluation of:
  – personal skills, expertise and aptitude;
  – personal attributes;
  – management skills;
  – the ability to deal with external factors.

2 INTRODUCTION

A small business enterprise is created as a result of a need in the market for a product or service. An entrepreneur is a person who identifies the need and develops a method of meeting the need. The method usually leads to the creation or expansion of a small business enterprise.

The relationship between an entrepreneur and a small business enterprise is that an entrepreneur **plans**, **establishes** and is **responsible** for the healthy **development and growth** of the enterprise. Not all enterprises are owned or managed by an entrepreneur, however. The entrepreneur and owner of the enterprise often appoints a manager to run an established small enterprise, or sells it to someone else.

An entrepreneur is always on the lookout for new opportunities, either in an existing enterprise or by creating a new enterprise.

Very often the consumer does not even realise that he/she needs the product or service. The entrepreneur develops the product or service and brings it to the attention of the consumer (marketing).

A small business manager is the person who manages and runs the small business enterprise. This person is responsible for the profitability of the enterprise and must have, learn and develop management skills.

Entrepreneurship is sometimes a feature of a small business manager, but not all small business managers are entrepreneurs. Similarly, not all entrepreneurs are small business managers.

Either an entrepreneur or a small business manager can be the owner of an enterprise.

DEFINITIONS OF AN ENTREPRENEUR

Definitions of entrepreneurs are similar, but they emphasise different features. The following are some of the definitions found in management dictionaries and textbooks for the term 'entrepreneur'.

Entrepreneurs are skilled at identifying new products, new methods of production or new ways of marketing existing products. They set up operations to provide new products, market the products and arrange the financing of the operations.

Another description is that entrepreneurs recognise opportunities for new products or services and get the finance and other resources to produce and deliver them. The finance and other resources may come from themselves or from other sources. Entrepreneurs are inclined to take risks and are generally associated with economic growth.

Both of these definitions imply **innovation** (in other words, that something new is created) because new products, services and/or methods are elements of the definitions.

In contrast, there is no reference to innovation in the following definitions. These definitions regard **establishing a new enterprise** as sufficient to classify a person as an entrepreneur.

> **Entrepreneurs are people with the ability to create an enterprise where none existed before. They produce combinations of ideas, skills, money, equipment and markets that form a successful enterprise.**

The more comprehensive definition of an entrepreneur given by Timmons *et al.* (1990:5–6) also does not refer to innovation or to a new enterprise as such, but to an entrepreneur's **creativity and aptitude for identifying and implementing opportunities**.

> **'Entrepreneurship is creating and building something of value from practically nothing. That is, entrepreneurship is the process of creating or seizing an opportunity and pursuing it regardless of the resources currently controlled. Entrepreneurship involves the definition, creation, and distribution of value and benefits to individuals, groups, organisations, and society. Entrepreneurship is very rarely a get-rich-quick proposition; rather it is one of building long-term value and durable cash flow streams.'**

There is evidently considerable agreement between the various definitions of an entrepreneur, though some definitions are more comprehensive or specific than others.

An entrepreneur can be described as someone:
- who starts an own enterprise;
- who manages an own enterprise;
- who identifies new products or opportunities;
- who is creative and/or innovative;
- who organises and controls resources (like capital, labour, materials) to ensure a profit;
- with the ability and insight to market, produce and finance a service or product;
- who has financial means or who can obtain financing so as to realise the enterprise;
- who is willing to take calculated risks.

This summary of the general definitions of an entrepreneur clearly indicates the role of an entrepreneur in **establishing** and **running** an enterprise. The summary therefore states what an entrepreneur **does** and gives a broad indication of the **characteristics** of an entrepreneur.

Answer the following by filling in only the missing words:
An entrepreneur identifies an .... in the market for a .... or .... and then develops a ....
to satisfy the need. An entrepreneur is therefore constantly in search of new .... and is prepared to take calculated ....

THE RELATIONSHIP BETWEEN ENTREPRENEURSHIP AND SMALL BUSINESS MANAGEMENT

The definitions and research on entrepreneurship reveal relatively conflicting perceptions, especially regarding **creativity** and **innovation**. On the one hand, only someone who starts and operates a highly creative and innovative enterprise is regarded as an entrepreneur. This perception implies that the enterprise must be different from any existing enterprise and that a person is an entrepreneur only if he/she acts innovatively. A more general view is that a person who starts and establishes any enterprise, not necessarily a highly innovative enterprise, is an entrepreneur. Once the enterprise is established, the person is no longer an entrepreneur, but is in fact a manager of the enterprise, or rather a **small business manager**.

People who are responsible for the **growth** of an enterprise are also iden-tified as entrepreneurs in terms of more recent definitions. 'Indeed, it has been suggested that growth may be a useful way to distinguish between small business owners and entrepreneurs' (Merz *et al.*, 1994:48).

Therefore, entrepreneurs are also small business managers, as they manage their enterprises themselves to ensure permanence and growth.

According to this definition, all small business managers and owners of small business enterprises are entrepreneurs. If a person does not display entrepreneurship by starting an enterprise or causing it to grow, she/he has not distinguished her/himself as an entrepreneur. This is a false perception.

Examples of small business managers who are not entrepre-neurs are:
- ❏ a person who manages an existing enterprise or franchise without ensuring growth;
- ❏ a person who inherits an enterprise and runs it in the same way as her/his predecessor;
- ❏ a person who is appointed by the owner of a small business enterprise to manage the enterprise.

Successful entrepreneurs realise that effective management is necessary for the success of an enterprise. They therefore manage their enterprises themselves or appoint small business managers to ensure permanence and growth.

The role of the small business manager in the enterprise is just as impor-tant as the role of the entrepreneur. An enterprise must be managed well to guarantee **survival** and **profitability**. Without proper management, entrepreneurship is meaningless, and even the best product or service in the world cannot ensure success. A successful entrepreneur will realise that if she/he cannot perform all the management functions properly, experts and/or managers must be appointed.

Thus, entrepreneurs are not necessarily small business managers, and small business managers are not all entrepreneurs.

Nando's
Robert Brozin and Fernando Duarte

Robert Brozin and Fernando Duarte, Nando's namesake, started the business. Brozin worked at Sanyo and knew nothing about the food industry, while Fernando Duarte was the food specialist.

Nando's started as a fast food shop selling spicy, grilled chicken meals in the south of Johannesburg in 1995. Mainly Portuguese people lived in the area and they enjoyed the typical Portuguese style of food. The business grew fast and the shop was often difficult to enter due to its popularity. Soon another Nando's was opened in the north and more affluent part of Johannesburg.

Today there are 343 Nando's worldwide. Of the total number, 184 are franchises, 70 are owned by Nando's and 159 are international, mainly in Britain and Australia. Success in the Middle East, however, is still a problem.

Nando's is well known and popular for its quirky, fun and cheeky advertising. Although the perception is that Nando's spends large amounts on advertising, due to the high visibility and its exceptional character, the annual amount spent is only R17 million, which is much lower than the budgets of the big players. This means that they have to be, and certainly are, innovative. Brozin describes himself as a people-orientated marketer.

The international operations already afford Nando's 57% of its earnings and the goal is to grow it to 70%. However, the SA market is close to becoming saturated.

Brozin acknowledges that the process of internationalisation is difficult. They've had quite a number of serious setbacks and he admits that they haven't always acted correctly and probably internationalised too soon. The learning curve in Australia was very steep and they realised that they could not dictate to the business climate, but needed to adapt to it. Today they are proud of their results in Australia.

The most controversial aspect, apart from their advertisements, is probably their loan position. The extensive international expansion created a loan to equity ratio of more than 100%. Over the last six-month period before August 31, 2000 it was brought down to 69%. Brozin attributes

☞

this result to the success with internationalisation. The profit for the last six months of 2001 was R2,6 million in Britain and R7 million in Australia. They are now experienced and known in those markets and Brozin is determined to extend the international expansion of Nando's.

Adapted from 'Die hoender kom hier beslis eerste'. 2001. *Sakebeeld*, Maandag 12 November, p.2.

Innovation, creativity and certain other typical characteristics of entrepreneurs are not needed for a person to run a franchise successfully. Proven directives govern the management of the franchise, so even a relatively inexperienced person could operate a Nando's effectively, given the guidance and experience of the franchisors.

The success of a franchise is determined by factors such as:

❑ the management skills of the small business manager;
❑ how well the directives are followed;
❑ the initiative shown to satisfy clients, like marketing individual spazas more effectively, providing better service by paying attention to the appearance and neatness of the unit, and a conscious policy of intensified customer service.

Management is a function of small business managers, but is not successfully performed by all managers. **An entrepreneur must therefore be committed to developing both entrepreneurship and management skills, as these are the things that contribute most to success.**

Thomas Edison, one of the greatest inventors of the nineteenth century, is a striking example of someone who was an excellent entrepreneur, but who did not know how to manage an enterprise properly.

Edison's ambition was to be a successful businessman and eventually the head of a large enterprise. He had all the knowledge necessary to found an enterprise for developing his greatest invention, the light bulb. His product was unique and led to a new consumer need. But Edison made a single mistake, namely remaining an entrepreneur without developing his management skills. As a result, his four or five enterprises all failed, and could be rescued only by a true management team.

An **intrapreneur** is an entrepreneur who has no need to start his/her own enterprise, but **wishes to use his/her business abilities in an existing enterprise.** In other words, an intrapreneur is someone who prefers the benefits of an existing enterprise (such as a regular salary and available resources) to the uncertainties of an enterprise of his/her own.

Intrapreneurship involves identifying an opportunity within an existing enterprise, and creating a profitable reality for the enterprise from this opportunity.

Some definitions are given in the first column of the table. Decide who they describe and in the second column fill in **entrepreneur**, **intrapreneur**, and/or **small business manager**.

DEFINITIONS	DESCRIBES ...
1. Must be committed to the development of entrepreneurship and management.	1.
2. Makes use of business abilities within an existing enterprise.	2.
3. Not necessarily a small business manager.	3.
4. Appointed to manage a small business enterprise.	4.
5. Runs own enterprises to ensure permanence and growth.	5.

5   KEY SUCCESS FACTORS OF ENTREPRENEURS

Entrepreneurs possess particular features that set them apart from people who are not intent on starting an enterprise of their own. This does not mean that all entrepreneurs have the same characteristics or combination of characteristics. Some entrepreneurs are successful because they are prepared to take chances, while others achieve their goals largely as a result of their innovative skills and flair for management. Each entrepreneur has a unique combination of factors at her/his disposal for achieving success.

Factors that usually contribute to successful entrepreneurship are known as key success factors, and can be summarised as follows:

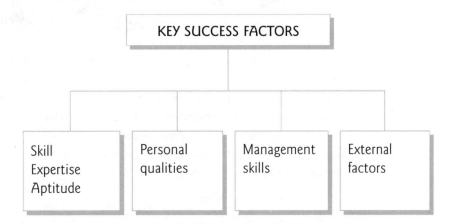

Before we examine the individual key success factors, let us look at the **profile of an entrepreneur**.

The profile of an entrepreneur is an indication of the personal **abilities** and **characteristics** the entrepreneur possesses. Considerable research has been done to try and describe a typical entrepreneur. However, the findings have shown that there is no typical entrepreneur.

Peter Drucker, the well-known management consultant and author, has said the following about the profile of an entrepreneur: 'Some are eccentrics, others painfully correct conformists; some are fat, and some are lean; some are worriers, some relaxed; some drink quite heavily, others are total abstainers; some are persons of great charm and warmth, some have no more personality than a frozen mackerel' (Drucker, 1966:22).

Few, if any, entrepreneurs possess all the key success factors that have been identified by researchers. In the next section, we will discuss the most important of these personal characteristics and management skills. Through his/her **introspection** and **self-evaluation** the entrepreneur can then establish what his/her personal strengths and weaknesses are. Strengths can be positively applied and weaknesses can be addressed by one or more of the following:

- ❑ personal development;
- ❑ attending courses;
- ❑ appointing staff and/or experts to compensate for the inadequacies of the entrepreneur.

5.1 The skills, expertise and aptitudes of an entrepreneur

Successful entrepreneurs have particular skills, expertise and aptitudes that can be applied profitably in any enterprise. It is best to start or run an enterprise in something you feel comfortable with and know a lot about (expertise) and/or in which you are skilled. The match between you, the person starting the enterprise, and the type of enterprise is therefore most important.

Skills usually refer to manual work, and can be learned. You can learn to become an electrician, a hairdresser, cabinet-maker, etc.

Expertise is based on knowledge that you acquire. Expertise and knowledge are obtained by **studying** and/or **experience**. There are experts in fields such as taxation, computer systems and study techniques.

Each person is also born with **aptitudes and talents**. Some are artistic, some have a talent for communicating, and others have a flair for figures.

Usually, your skills, expertise and knowledge are a product of your natural aptitudes, talents and interests. Someone who has a strong verbal aptitude, for example, will learn languages easily and so develop a sound knowledge of languages with further study. People who are artistic can practise art as a career or a hobby. They can paint or do graphic design. Further study can enable them to qualify in architecture or jewellery design.

The following are examples of ways in which an entrepreneur can use her/his aptitudes, expertise and skills in specific enterprises:

SKILLS, EXPERTISE OR APTITUDE	TYPES OF ENTERPRISE
1. Technical thinking (aptitude) + Cabinet-maker (skill) + Knowledge of antiques (expertise)	→ Draws furniture designs → Designs and installs kitchens and built-in cupboards → Restores antique furniture
2. Artistic (aptitude) + Experience in jewellery design (expertise) + Apprentice in jewellery manufacture (skill)	→ Produces and/or sells art → Designs jewellery → Manufactures jewellery
3. Analytic, practical thinking (aptitude) + Experience in stock control (expertise) +	→ Develops computer programs → Develops methods of stock control for enterprises ☞

Knowledge of book retailing, and of the need for reliable suppliers (skill)	→ Central distribution service for suppliers of books to retail shops

You can see how important it is for an entrepreneur to consider his/her skills, expertise and aptitudes when considering starting an enterprise.

1. Evaluate yourself critically and name your:

Aptitudes and talents	Skills	Expertise
....	....	....
....	....	....
....	....	....
....	....	....
....	....	....

2. List possibilities for you to apply your combination of personal aptitudes and talents, skills and expertise in enterprises:

....

....

5.2 The important personal characteristics of entrepreneurs

Expertise, skills and aptitudes in isolation do not guarantee a successful enterprise. To ensure success in your own enterprise, business characteristics and management skills are indispensable.

A successful interior decorator must have a thorough knowledge of materials, furniture styles and the use of space. Knowledge of various manufacturers and

their products and services is also essential. Such a person must also be artistic and creative, with a feel for colour and dimensions to furnish a room tastefully. These are the person's expertise and talents.

The interior decorator must also maintain **sound human relations**, as he/she will largely deal with people (clients, employees, suppliers and the public) when the enterprise is marketed.

Involvement in the enterprise ensures that the entrepreneur will use his/her expertise and talents to offer clients the best possible service. This in turn ensures the success of the enterprise.

This is an example of important **personal characteristics** displayed by successful entrepreneurs. The following are personal characteristics that warrant attention:

(a) Persistence

Entrepreneurs have confidence in themselves and their enterprises and **carry on** in spite of setbacks and difficult situations and problems. They are able to make immediate decisions, but can also exercise patience until a task has been completed and **a goal has been reached**. They do not lose heart when they make mistakes or fail.

'**Decisiveness, urgency and patience. Entrepreneurs must be able both to make immediate decisions and to take a longer view, sticking patiently to the task until they have realised their goals**' (Timmons *et al.*, 1985:81).

'**They all made mistakes and they all had setbacks, but they all kept going. Persistence, or perseverance if you like, is one of the qualities all these people (successful people) share**' (Marsh, 1992:8).

(b) Commitment to the enterprise

Entrepreneurs dedicate all their skills, expertise and resources to establishing and building the enterprise. They **prove their commitment** by:

❑ using their own money in the enterprise;
❑ taking a mortgage on a house;
❑ working long hours for the sake of the success of the enterprise;
❑ initially accepting a lower standard of living;
❑ possibly earning little or no income from the enterprise.

(c) Involvement in the enterprise

Entrepreneurs are personally involved in the enterprise and are aware of everything that is happening on **all levels** and in **all sections** of the enterprise. They perform tasks themselves and communicate with staff and others involved in the enterprise, such as suppliers and clients. The example of the interior decorator reminds us of the importance of personal involvement.

(d) Willingness to take risks

Entrepreneurs take **calculated** risks. This means that the risk related to a business opportunity must not be too great, for then the chance of success is not in the hands of the entrepreneur. They are not gamblers. The level of risk should not be too low either, as then exploiting the opportunity does not pose a challenge, and is usually not as profitable. A risk factor that is too low implies limited profitability. A business opportunity with a low risk factor makes it easy to enter the market, but also raises the likelihood of competition. In the business world this consideration is called 'barriers to entry'.

Entrepreneurs usually try to reduce risk by finding investors to provide finance, making arrangements with suppliers to provide goods on consignment, persuading suppliers of services and goods to accept special terms of payment, etc.

When a business opportunity is exploited, it must be done in a **carefully considered** and **planned** fashion.

(e) Sound human relations

Entrepreneurs have a close involvement with people. They realise they cannot be successful in isolation. They **motivate** their employees and know how to **build contacts** to the benefit of the enterprise. They find it important to ensure **long-term relationships** and stay on good terms with suppliers, clients and others involved in the enterprise.

'Human relations ability is demonstrated through such person-ality factors as emotional stability, skill in interpersonal relations, sociability, consideration of others, tactfulness, and empathy. For example, consider empathy. Empathy is the owner's ability to "put oneself in someone else's place" and know how the other person feels and perceives the situation. Thus, it is one of the most important facets of human relations ability in dealing with both customers and employees' (Pickle & Abrahamson, 1990:7).

(f) Creativity and innovative ability

Creativity refers to a person's imagination and **ability to think creatively**.

Innovative ability refers more to the **use** of creative abilities to **create something concrete**.

So it is logical that creative thinking, but especially innovative ability, is fundamental to starting a new enterprise.

Examples of creativity and innovation are:

❑ starting and expanding an enterprise by developing and marketing a **new product** or service, like a new computerised lawn mower that is automatically driven;

❑ presenting, marketing or making available an **existing product** or service in a **new, innovative manner,** for example MWeb, who provides a modem for Internet connection at a below market price (approximately 20% of the regular price) in a Big Black Box. MWeb thus ensures extended contracts with clients as they offer easy and cheap access to the Internet.

□ applying **new technology** to improve or extend an existing product or service, like 'Mr Delivery', which offers a home delivery service from a variety of restaurants.

Creativity distinguishes an entrepreneur from her/his competitors. Often it does not represent a radically new method, but it may be a method that satisfies a client's need in a better way.

(g) Positive attitude and approach

> **'Entrepreneurs use failure as a learning experience. The iterative, trial-and-error nature of becoming a successful entrepreneur makes serious setbacks and disappointments an integral part of the learning process. The most effective entrepreneurs are realistic enough to expect such difficulties. Furthermore, they do not become disappointed, discouraged, or depressed by a setback or failure. In adverse and difficult times, they look for opportunity. Many of them believe that they learn more from their early failures than from their early successes. They believe in their own ability' (Kuratko & Hodgetts, 1992:54).**

Entrepreneurs learn from their setbacks and failures. They are realistic and accept that disappointments are inevitable, and are not discouraged when these occur. They are able to identify opportunities even in adverse and difficult situations.

All this indicates that entrepreneurs remain positive despite setbacks, failure and disappointment. This does not mean they do not sometimes feel dispirited when events are not favourable, but on the whole they deal positively with situations. We often read of entrepreneurs who have lost everything, sometimes more than once, only to start afresh. **Success is achieved by using negative experiences positively and by learning from past mistakes.**

In this way, Henry Ford, father of the motor car assembly line and the first mass-produced motor car (the Model T Ford), twice started enterprises (both times building racing cars) that proved unsuccessful, before achieving success.

1. What are the two advantages an entrepreneur can enjoy by being personally involved in the business?

   (a) ....

   (b) ....

2. Entrepreneurs should not take risks impulsively, but they can take calculated risks. Why? ....

   ....

3. Is there a difference between creativity and innovative ability? Explain. ....

   ....

5.3 The important functional management skills of entrepreneurs

The management skills of an entrepreneur are an indication of how well the entrepreneur can perform important tasks or activities in an enterprise. Related activities are grouped, and are known as the **eight functions of an enterprise**. They are shown in the diagram on the next page.

*The functions are described in detail in Chapter 2. In Chapter 4 they are dealt with as part of the **viability study**, and in Chapter 5 they are applied as part of the business plan.*

In this section, which is about you, the entrepreneur, we discuss your ability to perform specific activities in the enterprise. You must be aware of your **strengths** and your **weaknesses** in terms of management skills in the various business functions so that you can apply or supplement them to build a successful enterprise.

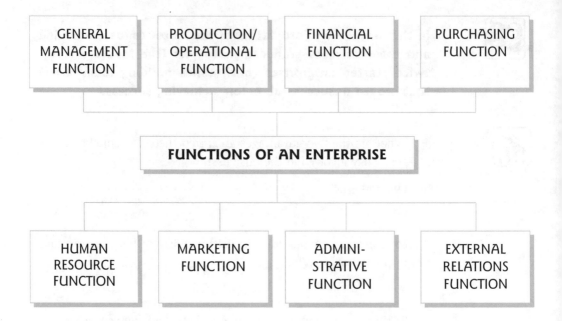

If you think back to the example of the interior decorator it is evident that the success of an enterprise demands specific management skills.

The interior decorator must be **market-oriented**. She must know which **target market** is to be served, for example:
❑ the higher income group or corporate clients;
❑ people with modern, traditional or alternative tastes.

The interior decorator must also be familiar with **marketing methods** and know how to reach the target market.

Managing and applying the **income and funds** is equally essential for the survival and profitability of the enterprise. If the interior decorator cannot manage her finances, she will have to get expert assistance.

According to management consultants, **marketing expertise** and **management expertise** are essential for the successful operation of small and medium enterprises (SME). Each successful entrepreneur should have a minimum or a particular combination of these management skills.

We will now look at the following important aspects of management skills:
(a) planning an enterprise before it is established;
(b) general management skills and the use of advisers;
(c) customer service;
(d) knowledge of competitors;
(e) market orientation;
(f) the importance of quality products/services;
(g) accounting for all purposes;
(h) insight into expenditure, income, profit and loss;
(i) the ability to use income judiciously.

(a) Planning an enterprise before it is established
This activity is part of the **general management function** and is part of the **drawing-up of the business plan**. A well-considered business plan ensures that the entrepreneur launches the enterprise with confidence, because it means the necessary research and planning have been done.

Entrepreneurs often do the planning very informally because they are in a situation where there is no time to draw up a formal business plan, or because they simply do not know how to do it. Despite their informal planning, these entrepreneurs are often successful.

Formal planning and drawing up a business plan are desirable activities, as they include the following benefits:

❑ By identifying problems early on, the entrepreneur can make wise decisions and fewer mistakes.

☞

- ❏ The entrepreneur is forced to take all the important factors concerning the intended enterprise into account, and is therefore less dependent on purely instinctive or crisis decisions. In this way, he/she avoids stress.
- ❏ He/she can take decisions for the future.
- ❏ The planning stage is an ideal opportunity for testing ideas.

A full discussion of, and guidance in, developing a business plan is given in Chapter 5.

(b) Possessing management skills and using advisers and/or experts where necessary

This activity is also part of the general **management function**.

Entrepreneurs know what is needed for success in a specific enterprise, and are intent on developing their skills in these critical areas of performance. If marketing the enterprise's products is the critical area of performance, and significantly determines the success of the enterprise, the entrepreneurs know how to do marketing. If they don't have the necessary expertise themselves, they appoint trained staff. They understand the environment in which they are competing and are well organised. Know-how is often more important than creativity.

As an entrepreneur, you will usually be aware of, or soon discover, your **weaknesses and strengths** in terms of the enterprise you are operating or intend to operate. It is **logical** that you will start a business in which you can use your expertise and skills (strengths).

Entrepreneurs must also be fully aware of management skills they do not have (weaknesses). These can be corrected by:

- ❏ using other people, like employees, consultants, contractors or professional experts;
- ❏ self-development and conscious efforts to make up for deficiencies by learning from others, attending courses, reading or studying.

The interior decorator knows that she is a very creative, artistic and stylish person. She realises that her financial knowledge is insufficient for her to do her own accounting, and so contracts her accounting out to an accountant. As a good businesswoman she accepts that she must be able to understand financial statements, and so takes a course to learn basic financial terms, concepts and principles to be able to take proper business decisions. She has identified her weaknesses, and is taking steps to avoid having her enterprise harmed by them.

(c) Customer service

This activity is included in the **marketing and administrative functions**.

Entrepreneurs who maintain good human relations are sensitive to clients' needs, and so provide very good customer service. Personal service is important. Examples are after-sales service; attention to details such as serving refreshments tastefully when a client visits the enterprise; personal presentability and attractive premises; user-friendliness like a neatly ordered shop and clear instructions on using products. Clients remember, support and recommend an enterprise that meets their needs and gives them something extra without making them feel they are paying for it. So, little gestures mean a lot: a balloon or sticker for the child; a cup of tea or glass of champagne in the jewellery store; changing an order on short notice; or just friendly, helpful service.

Administrative and technical factors are also crucial to sound customer service. Keeping records and filing systems for reference and stock control; a diary to ensure planning and keeping appointments; contract planning and target dates for completing projects; contracts; and job cards for information on clients are a few examples of methods that can help ensure effective customer service.

(d) Knowledge of competitors

This activity is also part of the **marketing function**.

Successful entrepreneurs know:

- [ ] who their competitors are;
- [ ] how many competitors they have;
- [ ] the size of their competitors' enterprises;
- [ ] the segment of the market their competitors control;
- [ ] the quality of their competitors' products/services;
- [ ] how to distinguish themselves from their competitors and so ensure and increase their share of the market;
- [ ] how to discover their competitors' strengths and weaknesses, and to convert a competitor's weakness into an opportunity for profit for their own enterprise.

An example is an entrepreneur who distinguishes her/his enterprise that sells Persian carpets, kilims and carrot cloths from similar shops by visiting clients at home or at work. She/he takes along a variety of suitable carpets and cloths to make the client's choice easier. The entrepreneur's professional know-how concerning the quality of the product and her/his taste and flair for colour (talent!) are presented to the client in a unique fashion. The majority of competitors sell their products from their shops or at auctions with no apparent interest in clients' homes or places of work.

(e) Market orientation

This activity is also part of the **marketing function**.

Successful entrepreneurs are market-oriented. They know who their target market is, what the **demands and needs of the target market** are and how to meet them profitably. The example of the interior decorator illustrates this functional skill. A market-conscious entrepreneur has developed products and services to satisfy the requirements of the client.

A market-conscious entrepreneur is positioned realistically towards competitors. This means that the entrepreneur's products and/or services are distinct from those of competitors to ensure profitability and a competitive edge. The consumer is the focus of the enterprise and products and/or services are developed and adapted to meet the client's wants.

Product-oriented entrepreneurs often have problems because they are more concerned with the product than the client, and consequently don't know how to market their products/services successfully.

The following quotation should serve as a warning:

> **'Many aspiring entrepreneurs are so in love with their product-service idea that they ignore the market; they assume it will sell ... The market road is strewn with product-service ideas that were heavily – and many times cleverly – advertised and went bust' (Burch, 1986:79).**

(f) Recognise the importance of quality products/services
This activity is part of the **marketing function** as well as the **purchasing function**.

Quality products are not necessarily expensive products. But the client does expect the quality of the product to be in keeping with the price charged. **Value for money** is important. A successful entrepreneur aims to offer clients a quality product while still remaining **profitable**. Costs must be kept in check without affecting the quality of goods. Quality products and services contribute to marketing, as they generate new clients through personal recommendations by existing, satisfied clients.

(g) Book-keeping for your own purposes
This activity is part of the **administrative and financial function**.

Successful entrepreneurs realise that they must be able to understand their own accounting systems. **Simplicity** and **usefulness** are the most important features of such systems.

A simple system that suits the enterprise is essential. The entrepreneur must understand **what** has to be done and **why** it must be done so that the information it provides can be properly utilised.

If the size and complexity of an enterprise are such that the accounting cannot be done internally, a **qualified person** must be appointed to perform this function.

The usefulness of the information provided by the accounting system is of cardinal importance. The information obtained from the accounting system allows the entrepreneur to make decisions on how to improve the management of the enterprise. For the entrepreneur, the main purpose of accounting is to provide **insight** into the use of financial information.

The accounting must be simple enough not to demand too much time. However, it must be comprehensive enough to ensure effective decision-making and management.

(h) Insight into costs, income, profit, loss, etc.
This activity is part of the **financial function**.

Successful entrepreneurs distinguish between income and profit. They realise that **income** must first be used to buy new stocks; to pay creditors, wages, salaries, tax and current expenses. Only once this has been done can the entrepreneur determine what portion of the remaining income or **profit** can be ploughed back into the enterprise and how much will be used for personal remuneration. The entrepreneur knows how to calculate profit and what it means to show a **loss**. She/he knows which costs are essential and understands the implication of increased **expenses**. This management skill is closely related to the next skill, namely the ability to apply income wisely.

(i) The ability to apply income wisely
This activity is also part of the **financial function**. We discussed this management skill in the example of the interior decorator.

The successful entrepreneur exercises **financial discipline** and understands what to spend money on and how it must be done to ensure success. An expensive motor car conveys an image of success, or may offer convenience to a client. If this is important to the enterprise, the entrepreneur will take the **risk** of buying the car. On the other hand, a successful entrepreneur will not waste money on unnecessary personal luxuries and status symbols.

Entrepreneurs must constantly take decisions on expenses. They possess and develop the ability to make the right decisions to ensure growth.

Examples of good decisions are:

❏ Sometimes paying a debt/creditor is postponed as long as possible to keep cash available for a special offer on necessary stocks, which will enhance profitability.

❏ Profits are applied within the enterprise instead of on holidays, luxuries and a more expensive house.

❏ Money is used in departments or on products that will result in the greatest profitability for the enterprise.

Remember that although all management skills are important, few if any entrepreneurs have **all** the management skills necessary to run a successful business.

Evaluate yourself by completing the following exercise:

Name the personal characteristics and management skills that are positive features of yourself. These are your strengths. Then name the personal characteristics that you feel you have to work on. These are your weaknesses.

My strengths ....

....

....

My weaknesses ....

....

....

....

5.4 Dealing with external factors that affect entrepreneurship

External factors and circumstances also influence the way an entrepreneur will be able to exploit her/his potential. How you **accommodate**, **deal with** and even **exploit** external factors to your personal advantage is a measure of your entrepreneurship.

As an entrepreneur you must be aware of the following external factors:

ECONOMIC CONDITIONS	The entrepreneur must know how to adapt to fluctuating interest rates or declining levels of consumer spending power.
TECHNOLOGICAL CHANGES	The entrepreneur must keep up with technological developments and know how to exploit them to the benefit of her/his enterprise.
SOCIAL AND CULTURAL FORCES	The entrepreneur must be able to identify opportunities for growth in market share following a rise in levels of education among large sections of the population.
POLITICAL AND LEGISLATIVE VARIABLES	The entrepreneur must realise the opportunities that arise after political adjustments and events.
PHYSICAL VARIABLES	The entrepreneur must keep abreast of the availability and price of resources, such as considering the use of alternative raw materials following price rises.
INTERNATIONAL FORCES	The entrepreneur who uses technologically advanced communications channels, for example, can expand to and even establish enterprises in other countries.

External factors are discussed fully in Chapter 2.

Skill, expertise and aptitude, personal characteristics and management skills determine the way a person will handle external factors. The relationship between a person's inherent attributes and external factors are crucial to successful entrepreneurship.

6 SUMMARY

All the factors that have been discussed must be analysed in personal terms. This may discourage some potential entrepreneurs, but it is vital that the aspiring businessperson be aware of all the important aspects. Remember that a successful entrepreneur is critical of her/himself, but **positive** about solving problems. The entrepreneur will therefore see which adjustments must be made or what can be done to start an enterprise that has been a dream. Thus the entrepreneur has a **vision**. She/he realises that it is essential to evaluate personal strengths and weaknesses **realistically** to achieve the goals.

7 SELF-EVALUATION

1. Think of enterprises in your neighbourhood. Give an example of an enterprise that is managed by (1) an entrepreneur and (2) a small business manager. Give three reasons why you think the first person is an entrepreneur, and the second a small business manager.

	ENTREPRENEUR	SMALL BUSINESS MANAGER
EXAMPLE OF ENTERPRISE		
REASONS	1. .... 2.	1. .... 2. ....

	3.	3. ....

2. Define the term entrepreneurship in your own words.

....

....

....

....

3. Name the four types of key success factors and explain briefly what each one means.

KEY SUCCESS FACTORS	EXPLANATION
1.	1. ....
2.	2. ....
3.	3. ....
4.	4. ....

4. Look at the analysis of your own strengths and weaknesses that you did in the text.

   (a) List the strengths and indicate how they will contribute to a planned enterprise or to one you are already involved in.

STRENGTHS	HOW STRENGTHS WILL BE EXPLOITED
1.	1. ....
2.	2. ....
3.	3. ....
4.	4. ....

(b) Now list the weaknesses and indicate how you will address them.

WEAKNESSES	HOW WEAKNESSES WILL BE ADDRESSED
1.	1. ....
2.	2. ....
3.	3. ....
4.	4. ....

5. Why is it important to take note of external factors when starting and managing an enterprise?

....

....

....

REFERENCES

Anon. 2001. Die hoender kom hier beslis eerste. *Sakebeeld*, 12 November, p.2.

Burch, J.G. 1986. *Entrepreneurship*. New York: John Wiley and Sons.

Drucker, P. 1996. *The Effective Executive*. New York: Harper and Row.

Kuratko, D.F. & Hodgetts, R.M. 1992. *Entrepreneurship: A Contemporary Approach*. 2nd edition. Fort Worth, Tx.: The Dryden Press.

Marsh, R. 1992. *Business Success in South Africa*. Cape Town: Struik.

Merz, G.R., Weber, P.B. & Laetz, V.B. Linking Small Business Management with Entrepreneurial Growth. October 1994. *Journal of Small Business Management*. Vol. 32. No. 4.

Pickle, H.B. & Abrahamson, R.L. 1990. *Small Business Management*. 5th edition. New York: John Wiley and Sons.

Tate, C.E., Cox J.F., Hoy F., Scarpello V. & Stewart W.W. 1992. *Small Business Management & Entrepreneurship*. Boston: PWS-Kent Publishing Company.

Timmons, J.A. 2000. *New Venture Creation: Entrepreneurship in the 21st Century*. 5th edition. Burr Ridge: Irwin.

BASIC BUSINESS CONCEPTS FOR THE PROSPECTIVE ENTREPRENEUR

2

1 LEARNING OBJECTIVES (OUTCOMES)

After you have studied this chapter, you should be able to:

- ❑ name the production factors and apply them in practice;
- ❑ indicate the relationship between the enterprise and the establishment and illustrate it by means of a diagram;
- ❑ practically explain the classification of enterprises and establishment in sectors;
- ❑ distinguish between the informal and formal enterprise;
- ❑ broadly discuss the forms of enterprise that are suitable for small business enterprises;
- ❑ identify the controllable variables in the micro environment;
- ❑ identify the controllable variables in the market environment;
- ❑ distinguish the various markets;
- ❑ distinguish between direct and indirect competitors;
- ❑ identify the uncontrollable variables in the macro environment.

2 INTRODUCTION

As we saw in the previous chapter, entrepreneurs are people who know their own weaknesses and strengths. If they lack the necessary expertise, they can call in other people to help. But entrepreneurs cannot depend totally on other people and must learn as much as possible about all aspects of their proposed enterprise. This includes learning the peculiar language and vocabulary of the business world to be able to communicate with their bank managers and other experts!

In this chapter and the next we will use Jaque Khumalo's enterprise as an example to illustrate the basic **concepts** and **principles** of the business world.

> The Khumalo family are some of the most successful small farmers in the Tzaneen district. After matriculating, Jaque (one of the daughters) went to the city to study domestic science. She returned disillusioned when she was unable to find work. Jaque immediately started helping with the farm, which produces litchis, mangos and other tropical fruit.
>
> Since the fruit is seasonal and the sale of the fruit is the family's chief source of income, it is hard going at certain times of the year. Jaque then hit on the idea of preserving fruit. In this way the family would have something to sell all year round, and so she could put her knowledge of domestic science to use. She started dreaming of an enterprise of her own, but realised that she needed more know-ledge of the business world.

Entrepreneurs are inclined, like Jaque, to start an enterprise with a **product idea**. Before she starts her enterprise, Jaque has to determine whether there are people with a **need** for preserved fruit. No enterprise can survive if there is no need for its products or services.

Entrepreneurs often make the mistake of developing products that do not meet the needs of consumers. Satisfied customers must be offered goods and services that have value to them, not just those that the small business owner thinks they will appreciate.

Satisfied consumers guarantee a successful enterprise.

People have almost unlimited needs, and their needs change constantly. Not everyone will need the specific fruit that Jaque wants to preserve. As an entrepreneur, you must always be aware of your consumers' needs and preferences. So you will continually have to find methods of satisfying their needs.

31

In Chapter 4 we look at a method of determining whether or not there is a need for a product and/or service.

1. Why should an entrepreneur know the vocabulary and language of the business world?

    ....

    ....

    ....

2. How can you, as an entrepreneur, make sure that your product or service meets the needs of the consumers?

    ....

    ....

    ....

3 PRODUCTION FACTORS AS RESOURCES WHEN STARTING AN ENTERPRISE

Jaque's desire to start an enterprise of her own is only the first step in establishing a business. She also needs money; she needs people who can help her; and she needs fruit to preserve. This shows that certain factors are needed to start an enterprise. These factors are known as the four **production factors**, and can be summarised as follows:

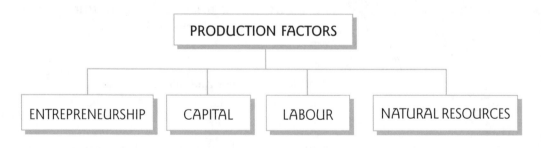

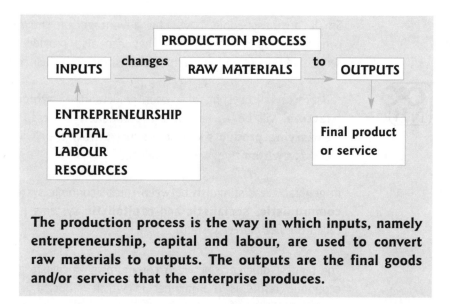

The production process is the way in which inputs, namely entrepreneurship, capital and labour, are used to convert raw materials to outputs. The outputs are the final goods and/or services that the enterprise produces.

❑ Capital (in this case **financial capital**) means the funds that Jaque needs for buying goods to use in the **production process**. Capital can also refer to the buildings, machinery and vehicles of an enterprise (**physical capital**), while it can also imply the technical knowledge and ingenuity of people who work in an enterprise (**human capital**).

❑ Jaque needs employees for specific tasks. These employees are her **labourers or human resources**. She pays them wages or salaries.

❑ The raw fruit that is needed for preserving comprises **natural resources**. Other natural resources include water, minerals, wood, leather and iron ore.

❑ Jaque's skill in combining the other three production factors, in order to generate a product, is known as her **entrepreneurial ability**.

These production factors are sometimes scarce. Jaque does not necessarily have the funds needed to start her enterprise. She cannot be certain that fruit will be available during the season (for instance, there could be drought). It is not easy to find expert staff. She might even lose her enthusiasm. Therefore she must exploit the available production factors to satisfy the almost unlimited and changing needs of consumers.

Entrepreneurs should offer **specialised or exceptional goods and services**. For this reason, the small business enterprise must concentrate on a relatively **select group of consumers**. In the business world this is known as **niche marketing**.

Small businesspeople have the advantage of knowing what their consumers' special needs are. They can also provide good after-sales service and maintain long-term relationships with their consumers.

> The economic system of a country determines **which production factors** will be applied in the production process, **which need-satisfying products** will be produced, **how** they will be produced, and **for whom** they will be produced.

In general, we distinguish between three economic systems, namely the **communistic, socialistic** and **capitalistic** systems (the latter is also called the *free market* system).

The biggest difference between communism, socialism and capitalism in economic terms is the manner in which property is possessed and controlled. None of the three systems is found in a pure form in any part of the world, but the economy of each country usually tends towards one of these three economic systems.

The most important aspect of the **free market system** is that entrepreneurs can start their own enterprises and make a profit. So entrepreneurs can take risks and compete freely with other enterprises. The smallest enterprise can compete with giant enterprises and still make a living.

1. Which four factors are needed to allow entrepreneurs such as Jaque to operate their enterprises?

   1. .... 3. ....

   2. .... 4. ....

2. Explain in your own words what niche marketing is.

   ....

   ....

3. Can an entrepreneur decide for him/herself how to apply the production factors? Give a reason for your answer.

   ....

   ....

☞

4. Can Jaque compete with other enterprises that preserve fruit (like KOO, Langeberg and Halls)? Give a reason for your answer.

....

....

THE ENTERPRISE, ITS ESTABLISHMENT AND THE SECTORS

Within the free market system the enterprise is an independent body that is established by an entrepreneur to provide goods and services that will meet the needs of consumers.

Jaque can adapt some of the buildings on the farm and use them for her business. The building she plans to use for canning the fruit is known as **the establishment** (factory or plant).

An establishment is the place where an enterprise's production equipment is found and where inputs (such as the raw fruit) are converted to outputs (such as the canned fruit).

In other words, an establishment can be regarded as the **factory** where the enterprise's products are manufactured. Although the activities in Jaque's enterprise are performed in different places, together they constitute her enterprise. **The enterprise comprises the establishment and all the activities that must be performed to provide a product and/or service** (see Figure 2.1).

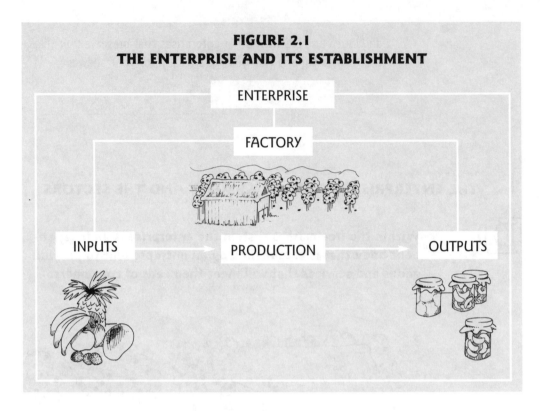

FIGURE 2.1
THE ENTERPRISE AND ITS ESTABLISHMENT

Enterprises and their establishments are classified in three sectors according to their activities, namely the **primary, secondary and tertiary sectors**.

❏ The **primary sector** is involved in *exploiting* natural resources in their raw unprocessed form. Jaque's father's fruit farm is a part of this sector.

❏ In the **secondary sector** natural resources are *processed and converted to a final product*. Jaque's proposed enterprise, which will process and preserve fruit, is part of the secondary sector.

❏ The **tertiary sector** is responsible for *conveying the final products* from the manufacturer to the consumer. The enterprises to which Jaque will sell her canned fruit for resale to the consumer belong to the tertiary sector. Major retail groups like Pick 'n Pay, Shoprite/Checkers and Woolworths fall within the tertiary sector.

1. The place where the enterprise's products are manufactured is known as the .... This place, together with all the other places where enterprise activities are performed, represents the ....

2. Complete the diagram below by filling in the three missing words in the outside circle.

3. Explain why the business Jaque wants to start will fall within the secondary sector.

....

....

....

....

5 PROFIT AND OTHER OBJECTIVES OF AN ENTREPRENEUR

Profit is a cornerstone of the free market system and an enterprise's **primary** (chief) objective.

> **Profit refers to a favourable difference between expenses and income (thus Income − Expenses = Profit). In this context we also refer to the profitability of the enterprise.**
>
> **Profitability (rate of return) is the net profit, for a specific period, expressed as a percentage of the capital that was needed to produce this profit.**

Profitability is important because it enables owners of small business enterprises to calculate the return on the capital invested in their enterprises. Their aim is to make this return as great as possible.

The primary objective of a small business enterprise is therefore to maximise the rate of return on capital (profitability) over a long period and direct all the activities of the enterprise towards achieving this objective. (For further information consult *Basic Principles of Financial Management for a Small Business* by A.A.C. Kritzinger and J.C.W. Fourie [Juta].)

> During the period 1/01/20XX to 31/12/20XX a cabinet-maker showed a profit of R5 000 on his small furniture enterprise. To make this profit he had to invest R50 000 in the enterprise by buying materials (wood, screws, glue, etc.) and new machinery.
>
> His profitability for the period 1/01/20XX to 31/12/20XX is 10% and is calculated as follows:
>
> $$\frac{\text{Profit during period}}{\text{Capital applied}}\% = \frac{5\ 000}{50\ 000} \times \frac{100}{1} = 10\%$$

Apart from the primary objective of an enterprise, the entrepreneur must formulate **secondary objectives** to support the primary objective.

Secondary objectives can include:

❏ the consistent provision of good-quality products and services to the consumer;
❏ creating favourable working conditions for the employees in the enterprise;
❏ maintaining cordial relations with the enterprise's suppliers.

How a small business enterprise will attain its primary and secondary objectives will depend on the type of enterprise (**informal** or **formal**) that the entrepreneur wants to establish.

INFORMAL AND FORMAL ENTERPRISES

An informal enterprise is an enterprise that does not have officially recognised business premises, which is not officially registered and does not keep official records.

A formal enterprise, conversely, is an enterprise that has a registered form of enterprise and is registered for tax purposes.

An **informal enterprise** is easy to start as it does not have to be registered or recorded for tax purposes. If Jaque decides to establish an informal enterprise, she cannot rent premises on behalf of her enterprise. Rental contracts require licences from the local municipality and an application to the local tax office for a tax number. It will also be very difficult for her to obtain finance and other resources. Financial institutions regard informal enterprises as **unreliable**, as they usually have **little security** to offer.

If Jaque decides to establish a **formal enterprise**, she will have to register a form of enterprise (such as a close corporation), obtain a tax number and comply with the local licensing laws and regulations. She will call her enterprise 'Jaque's Treats cc', and she will conduct all her transactions on behalf of the enterprise.

It is essential for each prospective small businessperson to have a knowledge of all the legal requirements that apply to her/his enterprise. A lawyer can be approached for advice. Statistics South Africa also provides information on formal forms of enterprise.

1. Complete the following:
    An entrepreneur must set objectives for the enterprise. The objectives consist of ...

    ❑ a primary objective, namely ....
    ❑ secondary objectives, namely (a) ....
                                                    (b) ....
                                                    (c) ....

2. Suppose you own an enterprise. In the first year you make a profit of R11 000. Calculate your profitability if you invested capital of R69 000 in the enterprise.* ....

    ....

    ....

3. What is the disadvantage of an informal enterprise for prospective entrepreneurs? ....

    ....

* The answer to question 2 is approximately 16%. Compare this with the example of the cabinet-maker in section 5.

7 FORMS OF ENTERPRISE FOR A SMALL BUSINESS ENTERPRISE

Entrepreneurs can choose from four forms of enterprise:

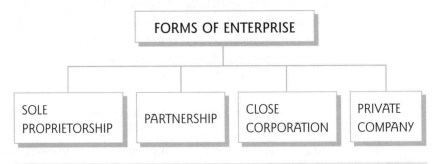

Factors to be considered when choosing a suitable form of enterprise include the following:

❑ The need to involve **third parties financially**. In other words: how great are the financial needs of the enterprise? If they are considerable, more people must be found who will invest money. ☞

☞

❑ **Legal requirements** in respect of establishing the enterprise and complying with regulations.
❑ The **expected ability** of the enterprise to exist independently of its owners. In other words: how long is the enterprise expected to last?
❑ The **liability** of the owners of the enterprise for debts, and their share of the profits. In some cases, the owner's assets are at risk if an enterprise fails.
❑ The **continuity** of the enterprise, including the extent of direct control.
❑ **The tax position** of the various forms of enterprise and how this will affect the owners.

We will now discuss briefly the various forms of enterprise.

SOLE PROPRIETORSHIP

A sole proprietorship is an enterprise that belongs to only one person and has no partners or co-owners. The owner can appoint people to work for him/her. He/she provides the capital, takes all the decisions alone, manages the enterprise and accepts all the responsibility for profits and debts. The lifetime of the enterprise is linked to that of the owner and there is no difference between private and business property. If the enterprise fails and there are debts, the creditors can attach the owner's personal assets.

Advantages
❑ From a legal point of view it is easy to start and to close down a sole proprietorship.
❑ All income belongs to the owner.
❑ The functioning of the enterprise is simple and can easily be adapted to changing circumstances.

Disadvantages
❑ The creditworthiness of the enterprise is limited to the assets of the owner.
❑ The owner is fully responsible for losses and can lose her/his private possessions if the enterprise should fail.
❑ If the owner dies, the enterprise may cease to exist.

❏ If it is sold or taken over, the enterprise no longer exists. This means that it must be founded legally from the beginning.

❏ The future of the enterprise is limited not only in terms of its establishment, but also in terms of expansion. A sole proprietorship can develop to a level where it exceeds the owner's capital means. If more capital is to be secured, then the form of the enterprise might have to be changed.

PARTNERSHIP

A partnership is formed when a group of people agree to combine their capital, labour, know-how and experience with the aim of making a profit.

A partnership comes into existence when at least two and not more than 20 people conclude an agreement. This contract, which should preferably be drawn up by an attorney, contains the names of the partners, the name and nature of the enterprise, the contributions (financial or otherwise), remuneration of the partners, division of profits and other aspects. It is important to choose partners carefully, and the partnership agreement must be drawn up with great care.

Advantages

❏ A partnership pools the management techniques, judgement and special characteristics of a number of people.

❏ Opportunities for obtaining capital are usually favourable and each partner can contribute to the capital of the enterprise.

❏ The legal requirements, such as a partnership agreement, can be dealt with easily.

❏ In a partnership the partners are taxed in their personal capacity and not collectively, so the profit is shared and each partner's share is taxed separately.

Disadvantages

❏ It is not always easy to find suitable partners.

❏ Partners are jointly liable for the debts incurred by other partners.

❏ Each partner is simultaneously a principal and an agent of the enterprise, and can commit his/her partners by his/her actions (for example, by accumulating debts).

❑ The partnership is dissolved if there is any change in its composition. This means that the life expectancy of the partnership is uncertain.
❑ It is sometimes difficult for a partner to withdraw from an agreement.

CLOSE CORPORATION

The close corporation does not have shareholders, only members who all have an interest in the enterprise. This interest is expressed as a percentage of all the interests in the corporation. The total member interest must be 100% at all times.

At the time of founding the close corporation, each member must make a contribution in the form of money, movable or fixed assets, or services rendered in its establishment or operation. The extent of a member's interest does not have to be in proportion to that member's contribution.

Only private individuals may be members of a close corporation (companies, partnerships, societies and clubs are therefore excluded). The number of members is limited to 10. A member's interest may, subject to certain conditions, be transferred to others.

A close corporation's name ends with the abbreviation 'cc', and the word 'company' may not appear in the name. The close corporation's name, registration number and the names of members must appear on all business documents.

Advantages
❑ The law is simple and easy to comply with.
❑ The close corporation has a simple management and decision-making structure. Most decisions are taken informally.
❑ All members are part of the management and have a direct interest in the success of the enterprise.
❑ The close corporation has a legal personality (it can act in its own name) with all the benefits this involves, and this gives the enterprise continuity.
❑ The members are not taxed personally for the dividends they receive.

- ❏ An auditor does not have to be appointed, only an accounting officer.
- ❏ Annual general meetings are not mandatory.
- ❏ Any addendum to the original founding document can be added simply by registering the addendum.

Disadvantages

- ❏ The fact that a close corporation may have only 10 members can be a problem if the enterprise wishes to expand. It can cause the close corporation to be converted to a company.
- ❏ The close corporation can have financing problems, as the members have limited liability for the debts of the enterprise. This makes it difficult to obtain credit.
- ❏ If a member wishes to sell her/his interest, all the other members of the close corporation must give their consent.

PRIVATE COMPANY

The company is a legal person in its own right. In other words it has a 'life' independent of its shareholders. There are various kinds of companies, like the private company, the public company and the company limited by guarantee (such a company does not issue shares and is not profit-orientated). A private company is the most suitable for a small businessperson.

A private company, with a maximum of 50 shareholders, must be registered with the Registrar of Companies and is identified by the words '(Proprietary) Limited', or 'Pty (Ltd)', after its name.

A private company is required by law to prepare audited financial statements annually. This means the company must appoint a chartered accountant. The company may be established by either an attorney or a chartered accountant. All prescriptions relating to authority, liability, management, the sale of shares, remuneration or dividends, etc. are indicated in the Memorandum and Articles of Association. The company may commence operations only after registration with the Registrar of Companies. An annual levy is payable.

Directors can be prosecuted if legal requirements are not strictly met. The chartered accountant or attorney assists the company by ensuring that annual tax returns, etc. are submitted on time.

Advantages

❏ The company is a legal person on its own and therefore exists independently from its shareholders. This status overcomes some of the disadvantages of a sole proprietorship and a partnership.
❏ A company's shareholders have limited liability for the debts incurred by the company.
❏ Shares and therefore ownership can be transferred.
❏ The private company is free of many of the formalities required of a public company.
❏ The company and its members are taxed separately.

Disadvantages

❏ A private company must meet various extra costs, such as founding costs, annual subscriptions and the cost of issuing shares.
❏ There are extensive prescriptions for establishing and managing the company.
❏ The company's business is, as a result of the compulsory publication of its statements, constitution, etc., known to everyone, including its competitors.

Note the following questions that you and other entrepreneurs must ask yourselves before you choose an enterprise:

❏ Do I want to involve another person or persons in the enterprise?
❏ What are the legal requirements and regulations that must be met when starting the enterprise?
❏ Must the enterprise be able to exist independently of its owners?
❏ Do I want to be liable for the debts of the enterprise, and how must the profits be allocated?
❏ If I die, should the enterprise continue, and how will it function?
❏ What will my tax situation be?

1. What is the maximum number of members that each of the following forms of enterprise may have?

FORM OF ENTERPRISE	MAXIMUM MEMBERS
Sole proprietorship	....
Partnership	....
Close corporation	....
Private company	....

2. Name three disadvantages of a sole proprietorship.

   (a) ....

   (b) ....

   (c) ....

3.

> Peter Robinson, André Roux and Masiya Skozana decided to start a consultation enterprise for engineers, INGIKONS. It would cost R65 000 to get this enterprise going. Peter contributed R26 000, while André contributed R13 000 and Masiya contributed R19 500. To find the remaining R6 500, they asked Jan Malherbe (who has his own enterprise) to invest the amount in INGIKONS in exchange for a 10% interest in the enterprise.

3.1 What form of enterprise will be the most suitable for INGIKONS? Give two reasons for your answer.

....

....

....

....

....

☞

3.2 Indicate each person's contributions to and interest in the enterprise.

MEMBER	CONTRIBUTION OF INTEREST	PERCENTAGE
Peter	....	....
André	....	....
Masiya	....	....
Jan	R6 500	10%
TOTAL	R65 000	100%

4. In what circumstances would you consider starting a private company?

....

....

....

THE BUSINESS ENVIRONMENT

As an entrepreneur you should know that your small business enterprise cannot exist in isolation. Its activities are influenced by certain **controllable** and **uncontrollable** variables. These variables occur in the environment in which your small business enterprise functions. This is called the **business environment**.

> **The business environment comprises all the factors that can positively and/or negatively affect the establishment, growth and survival of an enterprise. The business environment therefore promotes or impedes the enterprise objectives.**

As an entrepreneur you should also be aware of the variables (events) in your business environment, since they can present certain **opportunities** and **threats** to your enterprise. The business environment is also changing all the time, and factors that are significant today may be irrelevant tomorrow.

47

The small business enterprise has an internal and an external business environment. The **internal environment** constitutes the enterprise itself, which we call the **micro environment**. The **external environment** is the part of the business environment outside the enterprise. It consists of the **market** and the **macro environments**.

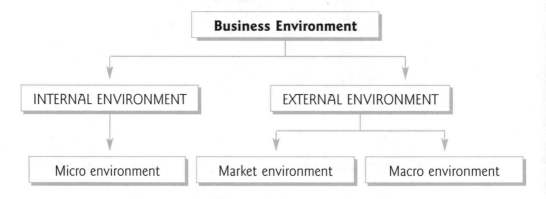

8.1 The micro environment

The micro environment consists of all the variables and factors that occur internally in the enterprise and which the entrepreneur can control.

Variables and factors that are important here are:

❑ the mission and objectives of the enterprise;
❑ the enterprise functions;
❑ the production factors.

THE MISSION AND OBJECTIVES OF THE ENTERPRISE
The mission and objectives of your enterprise are in broad terms **what** you want to achieve with your small business enterprise and **how** you will achieve it. (See also Chapter 4.)

THE ENTERPRISE FUNCTIONS
A great variety of activities occur within a small business enterprise in the process of providing goods and/or services. These activities can be systematically divided into smaller groups by placing similar activities together. Each group of activities is called a **function**.

We can identify eight interdependent main functions.

Can you still remember the eight functions of an enterprise?

Turn back to Chapter 1, if necessary, and complete the following:

```
┌──────────┐  ┌──────────┐  ┌──────────┐  ┌──────────┐
│          │  │          │  │          │  │          │
└──────────┘  └──────────┘  └──────────┘  └──────────┘

        ┌──────────────────────────────────┐
        │    FUNCTIONS OF AN ENTERPRISE     │
        └──────────────────────────────────┘

┌──────────┐  ┌──────────┐  ┌──────────┐  ┌──────────┐
│          │  │          │  │          │  │          │
└──────────┘  └──────────┘  └──────────┘  └──────────┘
```

(a) The general management function

The general management function includes all the activities that are performed in a small business enterprise to enable the enterprise to **attain its goals**.

These activities consist of four real elements:

The general management function differs from the others in that elements of this function are found in each of the functions of the enterprise. For example, if Jaque should appoint another person to market the canned fruit, this person's duties would include managing the employees working under him/her (the sales staff).

(b) The production/operational function

The operational function is concerned with the **conversion of inputs** (such as natural resources, labour and capital) **into outputs** (tangible products or intangible services). The person responsible for this function must plan, organise, co-ordinate and control the process so that a product or service of the proper quality is provided in the right place at the right time to the right consumer.

(c) The financial function

Activities in the financial function concern decisions on effectively **applying funds** and the best possible **use of sources of finance**. One of the chief reasons that small enterprises fail is their inability to plan and control their finances properly. Many small business enterprises are only aware six months after the end of the financial year what their financial position was on 28 February. This often has harmful effects for the enterprise.

(d) The purchasing function

To operate properly, all enterprises need **goods** like raw materials, equipment and machinery, as well as **services** like maintenance, installation and transport. The purchasing function is responsible for purchasing goods and services of the right quality, in the right quantities, at the right time, at the right price from the right supplier and delivered to the proper destination. Jaque's enterprise must, for example, buy sugar and containers to preserve fruit.

(e) The human resources function

The human resources function is responsible for the **effective use** of a competent, motivated **labour force**. This enables the small business enterprise to achieve its objectives.

(f) The marketing function

The marketing function embraces all the activities for transferring a product and/or service **from the manufacturer or supplier to the consumer**. The activities in the marketing function start and end with the consumer. First the enterprise identifies the needs of the consumer; then it provides a product or service that meets those needs (see Chapter 4).

(g) The administrative/information function

The administrative function comprises the **control of the information systems** within the enterprise. This extremely important function relates to obtaining, processing and making available information for the management of the small business enterprise. This enables management to take effective decisions to achieve its objectives.

(h) The external relations function

The external relations function includes all the things that are done to **promote the enterprise's image** in the external environment. This ensures that the people who are important to the enterprise have a favourable impression of the enterprise.

Few small business enterprises can afford to allocate one person for one function only. Typically, each person must fulfil many functions. Jaque can, for example, be personally responsible for the purchasing, administrative, and human resources functions. She can appoint someone to perform the marketing and external relations functions. She could use a book-keeper or an auditor for the financial function.

The enterprise functions mutually influence each other. So it is important for sound co-operation to exist in the performance of the various enterprise functions. The goals set for the performance of each must be closely co-ordinated and integrated. This will ensure that the enterprise achieves its global objective.

(The enterprise functions are discussed further in later chapters.)

THE PRODUCTION FACTORS

The production factors are the resources that are available to a small business enterprise. Using these resources, the enterprise must exploit opportunities or ward off external threats. If Jaque has adequate capital, she can enter new markets with her preserved fruit. A shortage of capital can place her in a weaker position in relation to her competitors.

Can you still recall the four production factors? (Turn back to section 3 if you need to refresh your memory.)

1. ....   3. ....

2. ....   4. ....

8.2 The market environment

The market environment includes the enterprise, and refers to all the controllable variables and factors outside the enterprise that have a positive or negative influence on the enterprise.

The most significant variables in this environment are:

- ❑ the market (the consumer and her/his needs);
- ❑ the competitors;
- ❑ the suppliers.

THE MARKET

The market consists of the consumers at whom entrepreneurs aim their marketing efforts, and to whom they thus want to sell their products and/or goods. *(In section 2 certain aspects of the consumer's needs were discussed.)*

The word '**market**' does not refer to the physical marketplace. To a small business enterprise, the market means *all individuals, groups or institutions that have specific needs in terms of goods and/or services and are prepared to pay for them.* In fact, everyone who needs a product, and is prepared to buy that product, can be regarded as the market.

We can distinguish more than one kind of market:	
CONSUMER MARKET	The transactions that consumers conclude to buy food, clothes, etc.
GOVERNMENT MARKET	Governments also buy goods and services to perform their duties. The South African National Defence Force could, for example, decide to buy Jaque's canned fruit as a dessert for its soldiers.
RETAIL MARKET	This market buys finished goods to sell to individuals or other enterprises at a profit. Shoprite/Checkers buys canned fruit to resell to its customers at a profit.
INDUSTRIAL MARKET	In this market, goods and services are bought by enterprises and used in the manufacture of goods or the provision of services to the final consumer. Consol Glass is the industrial market from which Jaque buys her glass bottles.
INTERNATIONAL MARKET	This market exists outside the borders of a country and includes all overseas consumers, manufacturers, retailers and governments.

1. Name the three most important variables in the market environment.

   (a) ....

   (b) ....

   (c) ....

2. Explain how Jaque can service each of the following three markets:

CONSUMER MARKET	RETAIL MARKET	INTERNATIONAL MARKET
....	....	....
....	....	....
....	....	....
....	....	....
....	....	....
....	....	....

COMPETITORS

Various enterprises compete with each other in providing the same product/service to the consumer.

Competition occurs when each enterprise tries to persuade a consumer that its product/service is the best, and that for that reason the consumer should buy products and obtain services there only.

The small business entrepreneur must know precisely **what product** to offer **which market**. In this way Jaque can identify her **direct competition** (enterprises that also sell preserved tropical fruit) and her **indirect competitors** (other enterprises in the canned fruit manufacturing branch of industry). (*A* **branch of industry** *consists of all the enterprises and establishments that provide more or less the same product and/or service.*)

Competitors can present certain **threats** or **opportunities** to entrepreneurs. If one of Jaque's competitors uses packaging that is exceptionally attractive to the consumers, it can affect Jaque's enterprise adversely.

SUPPLIERS OF RESOURCES AND SERVICES

Small business enterprises do not necessarily have the raw materials and other resources needed to manufacture their products or provide their services. They use products and services sourced from other enterprises or institutions.

Entrepreneurs need raw materials, water, electricity, communications and capital, for example. The enterprises that supply these resources include Eskom, Telkom and financial institutions like banks. All these enterprises or institutions are known as the entrepreneur's **suppliers**.

1. Give an example of a **threat** and an **opportunity** that competitors present to you.

THREAT	OPPORTUNITY
....	....

2. Those that provide goods and/or services for use in the production process are called the ....

3. Give four examples of **suppliers** and the **resources** that they can provide to small business enterprises.

SUPPLIER	RESOURCE
Example: Consol Glass	Glass bottles
1.	1. ....
2.	2. ....
3.	3. ....
4.	4. ....

2.3 The macro environment

The macro environment includes the enterprise and the market environment, and consists of all the uncontrollable variables and factors outside the enterprise that have a favourable or adverse effect on the enterprise.

The most powerful forces in the macro environment include:

FORCES	DISCUSSION	EXAMPLE
ECONOMIC CONDITIONS	Economic conditions like inflation, interest rates, conjuncture fluctuations (up- and down-swings in the economy) and the economic growth rate all influence the amount of money that the consumer has to satisfy her/his needs. Therefore the economic conditions in a country influence the consumer's ability to buy products.	If a manufacturer of leather goods mainly serves the consumers in the higher income group, a downswing in the economy can adversely affect that enterprise. A small business enterprise that sells an essential item like bread can also benefit from a downswing in the economy as consumers will buy cheaper products.
TECHNOLOGICAL CHANGES	New technological developments can present certain opportunities, but also threats, to the small business enterprise.	Sterilisation techniques can make a dairy farmer's products uncom-petitive in terms of price if old technology is used (a threat). Advanced equipment can benefit a small enterprise that repairs motor cars (an opportunity).
SOCIAL AND CULTURAL FORCES	Entrepreneurs must keep pace with the changing social and cultural aspects of their market, and constantly ask themselves the following questions: 1. What constitutes the market? 2. Where is the market situated?	One of the most important social trends is the increase of working women. The small business-person who starts a home industry will turn this aspect into an opportunity if he/she offers a service that makes life easier for working women. ☞

☞	3. Do the consumers' needs and preferences change? 4. What is the level of development of the market? 5. What is the role of population growth in the market? 6. What about the longer life expectancy of the consumers?	
POLITICAL AND LEGAL VARIABLES	Political and legal changes influence the way the enterprise performs its activities.	Legal requirements the small enterprise must comply with include: 1. obtaining a business licence; 2. registering as a taxpayer; 3. complying with the Companies' Act; 4. health requirements set by the local authority.
PHYSICAL VARIABLES	Natural resources are not available in unlimited quantities, so the small business enterprise must manage them efficiently.	Water resources are limited in South Africa, so available water must be used economically. Pollution is another variable in this environment that can threaten human survival. The entrepreneur must be aware of this.
INTERNATIONAL FORCES	Factors in the international environment that can play a role in the growth and survival of a small business enterprise include: 1. new technology; 2. international politics; 3. the international economy.	A small businessperson who sells computer packages bought overseas will be aware of world trends in software. Selling outdated packages can cause the consumer to change to an outlet that sells the latest software.

Suppose you decide to start an enterprise that sells dress material imported from Zimbabwe. Explain the influence the following variables will have on your macro environment:

1. ECONOMIC CONDITIONS

   ....

   ....

2. TECHNOLOGICAL CHANGES

   ....

   ....

3. SOCIAL AND CULTURAL FORCES

   ....

   ....

4. POLITICAL AND LEGAL VARIABLES

   ....

   ....

5. PHYSICAL VARIABLES

   ....

   ....

6. INTERNATIONAL FORCES

   ....

   ....

SUMMARY

As a prospective entrepreneur, you must ensure that your product and/or service is aimed at the specific **needs** of your market. The way you use your available production factors to provide the product/service will determine whether you satisfactorily attain your **primary objective**, profit. The **form of enterprise** that you choose also has a considerable effect on your success. If you understand the opportunities and threats in your **business environment** (the macro, micro and market environments), then you will be better able to steer your enterprise to success.

10   SELF-EVALUATION

1. Which **economic system** allows entrepreneurs to start their own enterprises and to make a profit?

   ....

   ....

2. Certain **factors** are necessary to establish an enterprise. What are these factors called? Briefly describe them.

   ....

   ....

   ....

3. Enterprises and establishments are classified according to their activities as belonging to **sectors**. Explain the sectors briefly.

   ....

   ....

   ....

4. Define the **primary and secondary objectives** of the enterprise that you are planning.

   ....

   ....

   ....

5. Which **form of enterprise** will you select? Why will it be suitable for your purposes? What are the benefits and disadvantages of this form of enterprise?

   ....

   ....

6. Define the **business environment** of your enterprise by using the following figure: ☞

BUSINESS ENVIRONMENT

INTERNAL ENVIRONMENT

EXTERNAL ENVIRONMENT

MICRO ENVIRONMENT

MARKET ENVIRONMENT

MACRO ENVIRONMENT

Define a mission for your enterprise.

....
....
....

Define the market for your products or services.

....
....
....

Define the possible positive and negative influences of the following forces on your enterprise:

1. Economic ....
....
2. Technological ....
....
3. Social and cultural ....
....
4. Political and legal.............
....
5. Physical ....
....
6. International ....
....

Name and define the 8 functions of an enterprise.

1. ....
....
2. ....
....
3. ....
....
4. ....
....
5. ....
....
6. ....
....
7. ....
....
8. ....
....

Identify your:
1. Direct competitors
....
....
2. Indirect competitors
....
....

Name 4 suppliers and the resources that they provide:

	SUPPLIER	RESOURCE
1.	....	....
2.	....	....
3.	....	....
4.	....	....

11 REFERENCES

Cronje, G.J. de J., Neuland, E.W., Hugo, W.M.J., Van Reenen, M.J. 1990. *Introduction to Business Management.* 2nd edition. Pretoria: Southern.

Du Plessis, P.G. (ed.) 1989. *Applied Business Economics: An Introductory Survey.* Pretoria: HAUM.

Le Roux, E.E. *et al.* 1995. *Business management: A Practical Approach.* Johannesburg: Lexicon.

Marx, S., Rademeyer, W.F., Reynders, H.J.J. 1993. *Business Economics: Guidelines for Business Management.* Pretoria: J.L. van Schaik.

THE IDENTIFICATION OF FEASIBLE SMALL BUSINESS IDEAS

3

1 LEARNING OBJECTIVES (OUTCOMES)

After you have studied this chapter, you should be able to:

❑ identify the stages of setting up a small business;
❑ improve your creative attitude;
❑ use your skills, expertise and aptitude to create your own small business ideas;
❑ convert common needs into business ideas;
❑ convert existing problems into small business ideas;
❑ identify small business ideas from everyday activities;
❑ identify small business ideas from other sources;
❑ develop and define your idea;
❑ distinguish between non-feasible and feasible ideas.

2 INTRODUCTION

The setting-up of a small business enterprise can be divided into three main stages, namely the identification of feasible small business ideas (**the idea stage**), the investigation of the profitable exploitation of the feasible idea (the viability study) and the drawing-up of a business plan (**the planning stage**) and the implementation of the feasible and viable small business idea (**the implementation stage**). Figure 3.1 illustrates the three-stage process.

The three stages, as illustrated on the next page, form the theme of the rest of this book. In this chapter we will discuss the first stage, namely the identification of feasible small business ideas. Chapters 4 and 5 deal with the planning stage, and Chapter 6 looks at the implementation stage.

As a prospective entrepreneur, you have probably already thought of possible small business ideas, or you may still be looking for a good idea. In this chapter you will get the opportunity to identify and develop various ideas.

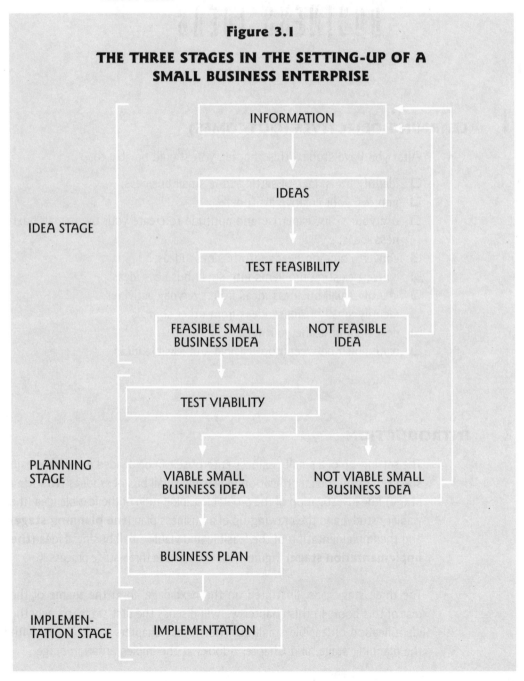

Figure 3.1

THE THREE STAGES IN THE SETTING-UP OF A SMALL BUSINESS ENTERPRISE

IDEA STAGE

INFORMATION

IDEAS

TEST FEASIBILITY

FEASIBLE SMALL BUSINESS IDEA

NOT FEASIBLE IDEA

PLANNING STAGE

TEST VIABILITY

VIABLE SMALL BUSINESS IDEA

NOT VIABLE SMALL BUSINESS IDEA

BUSINESS PLAN

IMPLEMEN-TATION STAGE

IMPLEMENTATION

The identification of small business ideas is a creative process. You must therefore be able to assume a creative attitude. All of us have the potential to think creatively. In this chapter you will be introduced to certain techniques which you can use to improve your creative mind-set.

Although it is important to think of as many small business ideas as possible, only one idea can eventually be converted to a small business enterprise. In this chapter we will help you to identify an idea that will be suitable for you (i.e. a feasible small business idea).

CULTIVATING A CREATIVE ATTITUDE

We saw in Chapter I that the capacity to act creatively and innovatively is one of the possible personality traits of an entrepreneur. Although an innovative small business idea can be very satisfying, it can also become a huge headache. It is not always easy to be first with a new product or service, because you must convince people that there is a need for your product or service. To be second or third means that you can learn from the mistakes of others.

This does not, however, imply that you should imitate others directly and offer the market something identical. As an entrepreneur, you should try to **provide specialised or exceptional products or services**. You must think, therefore, of small business ideas that will **distinguish** you from other competitive small businesses. To do this you must act **creatively**.

What is creativity?

> **Creativity is the ability to consider a topic in various ways and to come up with something new.**

Although some people are born with the gift of being creative, it is possible for anyone to **develop and improve** her/his creative abilities. It is important to understand that creativity is just as much an **attitude** as a manner of thinking. It is thus possible to think of new ideas by attuning yourself to creativity. You can use the following methods to improve your creativity:

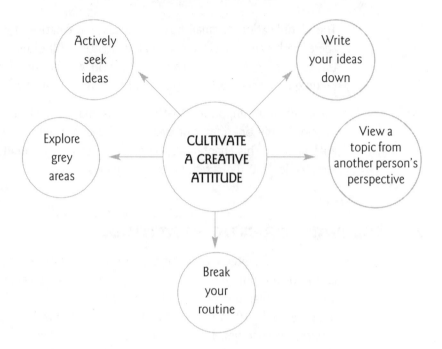

1. **Actively seek ideas:** You can learn to seek ideas actively by judging everything that you read or observe on the strength of the ideas that you can develop from it. If you think in this way regularly, it will become a habit, and ideas will come to you more easily.

2. **Write your ideas down:** Make a habit of writing down an idea as soon as you have one, even if you feel it is not a good idea. Regularly read through the ideas. This will give you the opportunity to review them, compare them with other ideas and perhaps combine them in a new concept.

3. **View a topic from another person's perspective/point of view:** If you put yourself in somebody else's position, you get a different perspective on a topic. With a better understanding of other people's points of view, you will gain new insights and ideas. By asking yourself, for example, what the mother of a pre-school child thinks of the concept 'to see red', and then looking at the same idea from the perspective of a busy businesswoman or a widowed grandmother, you can generate totally new ideas.

4. **Break your routine:** A good way of stimulating your thoughts is to break your routine. Here are a few suggestions:

❑ Take note of how you perform everyday actions, like washing the dishes, and do them differently.

❑ Spend a whole day without something that is a part of each day's routine, for example, your address book.

❑ Read a book on a subject that you know nothing about.

❑ Start a conversation with a stranger (someone you would not normally speak to).

❑ Do something you have never done before, like going to the opera, riding a horse or starting a new hobby or sport (in other words, broaden your horizons!).

5. **Explore the grey areas:** If you tend to see only the right and wrong sides of a case, it is time to explore the grey areas between right and wrong. Make a habit of looking for different solutions and possibilities. Start by completing the following incomplete questions. See how many solutions you can find to each in ten minutes.

❑ What will happen if I ... ?
❑ In what different way can I ... ?
❑ Who will benefit by ... ?

Take some time to tune your mind for creativity before you start looking for small business ideas. This mind-set will eventually help you to identify new or better small business ideas.

1. Define creativity in your own words:...

....

2 A creative attitude can be acquired by (fill in the missing words):

❑ Actively s .... g ideas.
❑ W ...... e down your ideas.
❑ S .... g a matter from a different perspective.
❑ B.................. g your routine.
❑ E .... e grey areas.

3. Consider all possible solutions to the problem of getting by without electricity for a whole working day: ....

....

....

4. Think of other ways to improve your creativity and write them
   down:*

   ....

   * You could use Dr. Kobus Neethling's book on creativity for this. See
   References for more details.

4 GENERATING SMALL BUSINESS IDEAS

A good idea seldom comes out of the blue – as an inspiration. As a
prospective entrepreneur you must deliberately **look creatively** for ideas
that can be converted into a small business.

In your search for small business ideas, you can make use of certain
techniques. The techniques for the generation of small business ideas
can be divided into five broad approaches:

THE GENERATION OF IDEAS				
FROM SKILLS, EXPERTISE AND APTITUDES	FROM COMMON NEEDS	FROM EXISTING PROBLEMS	FROM EVERYDAY ACTIVITIES	FROM OTHER SOURCES

There are various methods by which small business ideas can be identified
from the above sources. The approaches we use in this chapter have been
tested successfully and promise to produce positive results. We will
discuss the five approaches in the following sections.

4.1 The generation of ideas from the entrepreneur's skills, expertise and aptitude

We all have certain skills. In Chapter I we saw that an entrepreneur's
skills, expertise and aptitudes are some of the key factors for success.

**Turn back to Chapter I and take another look at your list of
entrepreneur's skills, expertise and aptitudes.**

In addition, consider the following:

❑ Formal training does not guarantee success in a small business enterprise. This does not mean that your qualifications are useless, however. Through your studies you can obtain certain knowledge which can lead to certain small business ideas. *An engineering student has, for example, gained certain technical knowledge which could give her/him the idea of starting a specific manufacturing business.*

❑ Skills can also be gained from working experience. As an employee you are responsible for certain activities. Your knowledge of these activities can enable you to start a business of your own involving these activities. *For example, the fact that you functioned in a marketing capacity can be the reason why you want to start an advertising agency or act as a marketing consultant.*

❑ Have you developed any skills through your hobbies or other non-career activities that you could use as ideas for your own business? *For example, the fact that you collect stamps, and know how to negotiate to get the best swap or price for your stamps, means you have learned certain purchasing or negotiating skills.*

Have you thought of new skills, expertise and aptitudes? If so, write them down, together with the skills, expertise and aptitudes that you listed in Chapter 1.

1. List the **skills** that you possess – for example, can do welding or knitting.

    ....

    ....

2. Identify your **expertise**:

FORMAL QUALIFICATIONS OBTAINED	EXPERIENCE GAINED
Example: National Diploma in Marketing	Example: Handling difficult customers
....	....
....	....
....	....
....	....

....

....

....

3. Write down your natural **aptitudes/talents** and **interests** (including hobbies)

   Example: Can communicate well (**aptitudes/talents**)

   ....

   ....

   ....

   ....

   Example: Woodwork (**interests**)

   ....

   ....

   ....

   ....

Your list of skills, expertise and aptitudes can now be used to identify small business ideas. To show you how this can be done, we will use Jaque as an example again. Jaque has one outstanding skill, namely that she can cook well. With this skill she can provide a product or service for individuals or organisations. You can identify many small business ideas by thinking of how to provide products or services to individuals or organisations, and what types of products or services they might need.

By doing the exercise on the following pages, you can see how many small business ideas Jaque, with her single skill, could identify. If Jaque could obtain all these ideas from only one skill, think of all the small business ideas that you could get with all your skills!

eg

(Adapted from: *The Ideas Generation Workbook* of the Scottish Enterprise Foundation)

WHICH SERVICE?
Cook relief service
Special diet recipe service
Conference meals

WHICH SERVICE?
'Cook for one' recipes
Cooking lessons
Wedding catering

FOR WHOM?
Restaurants
Guesthouses
Companies

FOR WHOM?
Old and single people
People who cannot cook well
Engaged couples

FOR ORGANISATIONS   **FOR INDIVIDUALS**

PROVIDE A SERVICE

START HERE:

SKILL:
Cook

MANUFACTURE A PRODUCT

FOR ORGANISATIONS   **FOR INDIVIDUALS**

FOR WHOM?
Hotels
Sweet shops
Bakeries

FOR WHOM?
Vegetarians
Diabetics
Children

WHICH PRODUCTS?
Frozen food
Home-made chocolate
Health bread/loaves

WHICH PRODUCTS?
Vegetarian dishes
Sugar-free cakes
Gingerbread figures

Take one of the skills that you listed and write it in the space in the middle. Think of individuals and organisations that can use a product or service that is related to your skill. Now think of all the various products or services that you can provide to individuals or organisations using this skill.

WHICH SERVICE?

WHICH SERVICE?

FOR WHOM?

FOR WHOM?

FOR ORGANISATIONS   **FOR INDIVIDUALS**

PROVIDE A SERVICE

START HERE: **SKILL:**

MANUFACTURE A PRODUCT

FOR ORGANISATIONS   **FOR INDIVIDUALS**

FOR WHOM?

FOR WHOM?

WHICH PRODUCTS?

WHICH PRODUCTS?

4.2 The generation of ideas from common needs

We all need something. However, our needs are not all the same. You must use your small business idea to try to satisfy a need among various people for the same product or service. In other words, you must try to satisfy a **common/shared** need.

Individuals with common needs can very often be grouped together; *for example, all mothers with small children, all members of a soccer team and all prospective homeowners have certain corresponding needs.*

You can also identify groups of **organisations** that have the same need. *Examples are businesses that need catering on a regular basis, or businesses that have a need for a complete maintenance service.*

Can you think of a few groups of individuals or organisations that have more or less the same needs? Write examples of interest groups and their needs in the spaces provided:

INTEREST GROUP	COMMON NEEDS
1.	1. ....
2.	2. ....
3.	3. ....
4.	4. ....
5.	5. ....

Suppose we regard cyclists as a group – those who ride bicycles for recreation. Write down the group's needs as you answer the questions on the opposite page. You can use the answers to develop new small business ideas.

(Adapted from: *The Ideas Generation Workbook of the Scottish Enterprise Foundation*)

Emergency repair service for cyclists

Clip-on umbrella

Trade-in handlebar replacement service

NOT EASY TO USE?
Tyre repair equipment

WANTS IT BUT IT DOES NOT EXIST?
Something to keep hair dry

OLD-FASHIONED?
Dropped handlebars

START HERE:

INTEREST GROUP:
Cyclists

KNOW ABOUT IT BUT CANNOT GET IT?
Purple cycling shorts

TOO EXPENSIVE?
Mountain bike

QUALITY IS NOT GOOD ENOUGH?
Steel handlebars rust in rain

Dye existing cycling shorts

Rental service for mountain bikes

Plastic-covered steel handlebars

By concentrating on the needs of only one interest group, you will find that many small business ideas will occur to you.

Take another one of the interest groups that you listed on page 72 and use the questions below to identify small business ideas.

NOT EASY TO USE?

WANTS IT BUT IT DOES NOT EXIST?

OLD-FASHIONED?

START HERE:

INTEREST GROUP:

KNOW ABOUT IT BUT CANNOT GET IT?

TOO EXPENSIVE?

QUALITY IS NOT GOOD ENOUGH?

4.3 The generation of ideas from existing problems

Instead of thinking of unfulfilled needs, you can think of existing unsolved problems. Think of things that irritate you or other people. Now think of ways of removing these irritations or frustrations.

Small businesses can, for example, buy only small quantities of stock at a time and must consequently pay higher prices than businesses that buy in bulk. An entrepreneur can solve this problem, for example, by acting as a part-time buyer for various small businesses and in this way obtain bulk prices for them.

Make a list of your problems and a list of problems that other people experience. (*Note that it is not worth the trouble to start a small enterprise that solves only one person's problem. Try to identify problems that affect various people.*)

❑ **Your problems**:
  Example: I've got big feet and have difficulty finding attractive shoes to buy...

  ....

  ....

  ....

  ....

❑ **Problems that other people experience:**
  Example: Litter/refuse dropped in the streets.............................

  ....

  ....

  ....

  ....

Knowledge of these problems enables you as a prospective entrepreneur to find the **initial idea** for a small enterprise that is based on the **solution** of a specific problem.

The technique that we will use is once again that of the Scottish Enterprise Foundation. If we take the general problem of *traffic jams* as an example, we can illustrate the technique as shown on the next page.

Cycles, train, bus, taxi	Videos on traffic lights Banners with useful information	Traffic queue minder service

SUBSTITUTE? Use another mode of transport	**SHIFT THE POINT OF FOCUS?** Entertain the driver	**RIDICULOUS SUGGESTIONS?** Leave the car in the queue

START HERE:

REDUCE THE PROBLEM? Fewer cars	**PROBLEM** Traffic jams	**MAKE IT BETTER?** Reduce the tension
Lift clubs		Car phone

LOOK AT IT FROM ANOTHER ANGLE Residents	**MAKE IT UNNECESSARY?** Do not travel	***RANDOM WORD ASSOCIATION?** Plants grow

Earn money washing cars while you wait in peak hours	Work and shop close to home	Roads grow – make more lanes available

* Use a dictionary or the Yellow Pages and choose any word. Let your mind roam from that word to a solution for the problem.

(Adapted from: *The Ideas Generation Workbook* of the Scottish Enterprise Foundation)

Take one of the problems that you listed on page 74 and use the same technique to identify small business ideas. Start by writing your problem in the middle of the diagram and then use the questions to think of new small business ideas.

SUBSTITUTE?

SHIFT THE POINT OF FOCUS?

RIDICULOUS SUGGESTIONS?

START HERE:

REDUCE THE PROBLEM?

PROBLEM

MAKE IT BETTER?

LOOK AT IT FROM ANOTHER ANGLE

MAKE IT UNNECESSARY?

RANDOM WORD ASSOCIATION?

4.4 The generation of ideas from everyday activities

You can identify many small business ideas merely by being aware of the activities that we perform daily. Use the following **methods** to identify ideas from everyday activities.

❑ **Use print or electronic media:** Think of the products that are advertised on television, in magazines and newspapers. Ask yourself whether they can be improved or distributed or marketed in a different way.

❑ **Look in other places:** You can come up with small business ideas by looking in unlikely places. Use the following questions to help:
- What ideas can you get at an airport; a movie theatre or a church?
- What ideas can you bring back from a sports meeting, a fun fair or a doctor's consulting rooms?
- 'Explore a part of your city or town that you have not seen before. What do you notice?
- Take note of the novelties and different ways of doing things at places where you go on holiday.

❑ **Talk to other people:** Have conversations with your family, friends, colleagues and businesspeople and find out if they have come across possible small business ideas. *The problem of obtaining holiday accommodation at short notice could, for example, lead to a small enterprise that specialises in finding and allocating unused and cancelled holiday accommodation.*

❑ **At work:** Ask yourself if the products and services that are used by the enterprise where you work could be improved. *The aerogram letter that is written on and at the same time serves as the envelope could possibly have been generated in this way.*

❑ **Going shopping:** Examine some of the products on your next visit to the shops. Remember that no product or service is perfect. By asking questions about the products, new ideas can emerge. Here are some questions to ask yourself:
- What problems are there with this product?
- How can the product be improved in any way?
- Is there a better way for the product to be packaged?

      – Can any new product be added to the present range of products?
      – Can the product be aimed at another market?

The child-proof lid, which is used on medicine bottles to prevent children opening the bottle, probably was developed after someone thought about the dangers of medicine bottles.

❑ **Changes in your immediate area:** By taking note of changes or important events that take place in your immediate area on a daily basis, you can also identify new business ideas. *If a South African sports team wins a championship or Olympic medal, this creates an opportunity for an entrepreneur to sell T-shirts bearing a suitable message.*

1. Which places have you visited recently?

....

....

2. Write down all the small business ideas that you could identify on your recent visits.

....

....

....

3. List 5 activities that you perform on a daily basis. Now think of possible small business ideas obtained from each activity and write these down in the next column.

DAILY ACTIVITIES	POSSIBLE SMALL BUSINESS IDEAS
1.	1. ....
2.	2. ....
3.	3. ....
4.	4. ....
5.	5. ....

4.5 The generation of ideas from other sources

Apart from taking note of everyday activities, you can also get ideas by consulting other reference sources. The following are some examples:

❑ **The Yellow Pages:** The Yellow Pages list almost all products and/or services that small businesses can provide. It is better to use the Yellow Pages of a large city, as it contains more information. By reading the reference index at the end of the Yellow Pages, you can discover a variety of products and/or services in a short space of time. The adverts in the Yellow Pages can provide more information on specific products and/or services.

❑ **Consult business publications:** Magazines like *Southern African Success: Southern Africa's Journal of Business Opportunities* can be a valuable source of small business ideas. The *Financial Mail* and *Finansies en Tegniek* are South African business magazines that carry weekly articles on successful entrepreneurs in South Africa.

❏ **Contact an inventors' association:** This can be a rich source of ideas; for example, you might be able to collaborate with an inventor to produce and market her/his invention. Two associations that might be useful to contact are the Institute of Inventors and the SA Inventors & Designer Society.

❏ **Examine overseas products:** Products that are not yet available in South Africa are often imported, imitated or adapted for the South African market. The franchise 'Sweets from Heaven', which presents a variety of sweets in a particular way, was based on an idea obtained from abroad.

❏ **Examine patents that have expired:** Patents that have expired are public property. There can be various reasons why a patent has not been exploited, and it may now be ready for the market. These reasons can include:
   - The market for this product has grown in the interim.
   - It can now be used with other products that were previously unavailable.
   - New technology now makes the manufacture of the product technically feasible and commercially viable.
   - A new use for the product has arisen.

An example of an expired patent is antibiotics and pills to alleviate muscular injuries. Lennon Medicines sell a product called Panamor that is comparable to the well-known product Voltaren. Panamor originated on the expiry of a patent on the original product.

❏ **Visit trade shows:** Trade shows are a good source of small business ideas. You also get the opportunity to see the product and to talk to the exhibitors about the market, product features, new technology and even the possibility of doing business together.

❏ **Investigate advertisements for small business opportunities:** Newspapers and magazines often carry advertisements for small business opportunities. Although many of these must be investigated with caution, there are real opportunities and these can serve as sources of new small business ideas. Note, for example, how many franchising opportunities are advertised in the newspapers!

1. Use one or more of the following sources and **write down** the small business ideas that you can identify from them.

SOURCE	SMALL BUSINESS IDEA
The Yellow Pages	....
Business magazines	....
Inventors' associations	....
Patents that have expired	....
Advertisements	....

2. Think of another 3 sources of small business ideas and write them down below.

    (a) ....

    (b) ....

    (c) ....

THE DEVELOPMENT AND EVALUATION OF SMALL BUSINESS IDEAS

In the previous section you were encouraged not to limit your creativity, but to think about all possible small business ideas. Most of these ideas will not work, however. The **initial sifting** of these ideas is performed by relying on your personal judgement and 'gut feeling'.

Now use your personal judgement and intuition and choose 10 possible small business ideas. **Write** these down below.

1. ....
2. ....
3. ....
4. ....
5. ....
6. ....
7. ....
8. ....
9. ....
10. ....

Only one of the small business ideas that you have listed can be converted into a small business on its own or in combination with one or more of the other ideas on your list. To choose the right small business idea, you must **evaluate** each of the ideas on your list.

Although there are examples of entrepreneurs who have, merely on the strength of their intuition, converted a small business idea into a successful small business opportunity, this is not the best way. *(Henry Ford, the creator of the Model T Ford, is an example of someone who followed his intuition and made millions from it.)* However, there are effective **methods** to evaluate small business ideas.

We evaluate small business ideas chiefly by means of two methods, namely a **feasibility study** and a **viability study**.

A feasibility study is a *general examination* of the potential of the idea to be converted into a small business enterprise. This study focuses largely on the ability of the entrepreneur to convert the idea into a small business enterprise.

A viability study is an *in-depth investigation* of the profitability of the idea to be converted into a small business enterprise.

Before you can start evaluating your small business idea, you must first be clear about what each of these ideas means. In particular, two things must be clear:

❑ what are the chief business activities?
❑ who are your consumers?

The **business activities** that you can perform with your small business idea will consist of two or more of the following:
❑ the manufacture of a product;
❑ the provision of a service;
❑ the sale of other people's products and/or services.

Your **consumers** will consist of:
❑ individuals, and/or
❑ organisations.

We can illustrate the possible business activities and consumers of a small business enterprise by means of the following 'bow-tie' diagram *(an idea taken from the workbook of the Scottish Enterprise Foundation):*

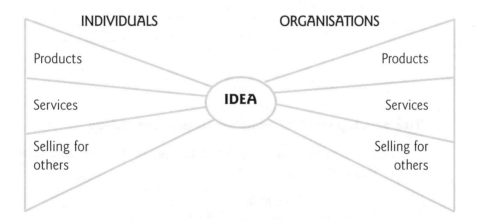

The 'bow-tie' diagram on the previous page provides **six options** for your business, namely:

1. the manufacture of products for individuals;
2. the provision of services for individuals;
3. the sale of other people's products and/or services to individuals;
4. the manufacture of products for organisations;
5. the provision of services for organisations;
6. the sale of other people's products and /or services to organisations.

Determine for yourself which option you will follow with a specific small business idea by performing the following actions:

1. Take one of the small business ideas that you listed and **position** it on the 'bow-tie' diagram on page 83, by making a cross at the place which represents the business activities and consumers of your idea. You can make notes on the diagram if you wish.

2. **Define** your chosen business idea in terms of its business activity and consumers.
   Example: *The sale of other people's products to organisations.*

   ....

   ....

   ....

5.1 The development of your small business ideas

The 'bow-tie' diagram can also be used to **develop** your small business idea in terms of the:

❑ essence of the idea;
❑ possible combination of ideas;
❑ taking a new direction with the idea.

Suppose we take the idea *'to bake cakes'*. In the following diagram you can see all the ideas that might emerge from this one idea.

(Adapted from: *The Ideas Generation Workbook* of the Scottish Enterprise Foundation)

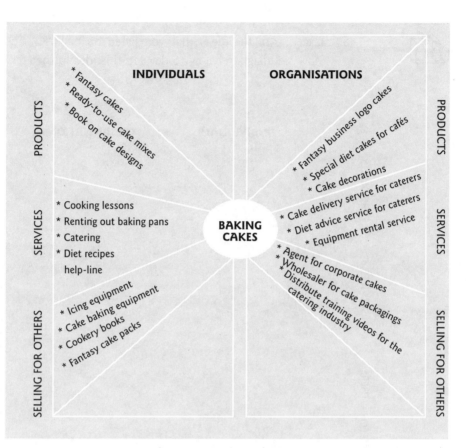

INDIVIDUALS

PRODUCTS
* Fantasy cakes
* Ready-to-use cake mixes
* Book on cake designs

SERVICES
* Cooking lessons
* Renting out baking pans
* Catering
* Diet recipes help-line

SELLING FOR OTHERS
* Icing equipment
* Cake baking equipment
* Cookery books
* Fantasy cake packs

BAKING CAKES

ORGANISATIONS

PRODUCTS
* Fantasy business logo cakes
* Special diet cakes for cafés
* Cake decorations

SERVICES
* Cake delivery service for caterers
* Diet advice service for caterers
* Equipment rental service

SELLING FOR OTHERS
* Agent for corporate cakes
* Wholesaler for cake packagings
* Distribute training videos for the catering industry

From the above exercise you can see that we can develop further the idea '*to bake cakes*'. Here are some examples:

❑ baking fantasy cakes (*the essence of the idea*);
❑ making fantasy cakes and making and selling cake decorations to bakeries (*the combination of ideas*);
❑ the distribution of training videos for the catering industry (*taking a new direction with the idea*).

1. Take one of the ideas that you listed on page 82, and use the 'bow-tie' diagram below to develop this idea further.

INDIVIDUALS   **ORGANISATIONS**

PRODUCTS   PRODUCTS

SERVICES   SERVICES

SELLING FOR OTHERS   SELLING FOR OTHERS

2. Explain how you will use the idea to do the following:

    (a) Determine the essence of your idea ....

    (b) Combine ideas ....

    (c) Take a new direction with an idea ....

5.2 The feasibility of your small business ideas

Can you still remember what is meant by a feasibility study? (By all means turn back to the explanation on page 82).

To determine whether your small business idea is feasible, you must be able to answer the following four questions satisfactorily (*as presented by the Scottish Enterprise Foundation*):

- ❑ Do you want to do what the idea suggests?
- ❑ Is there a market for your idea?
- ❑ Can you meet the needs of your consumers?
- ❑ Can you get the idea to the consumers?

To determine the feasibility of your small business idea, answer the following questions, by filling in a tick (✓) or a question mark (?) in the block alongside each question:

1. DO YOU WANT TO DO WHAT THE IDEA SUGGESTS?

- ☐ Is the idea really something that you want to pursue?
- ☐ Do you want to do business with the types of people who will be your customers?
- ☐ Do you have the health, energy and personality to pursue your idea?
- ☐ Can you cope with the long hours, few if any holidays, etc. associated with this idea?
- ☐ Will you sacrifice the things that are important to you in order to make a successful enterprise out of this idea?
- ☐ Does your family understand the full implications of your decision to start a small business?
- ☐ Do you have the support of your family and are they willing to help?
- ☐ Is this idea more important to you than any other idea that you have identified?

(Adapted from: *The Ideas Generation Workbook* of the Scottish Enterprise Foundation)

If you filled in any question marks (?) in the blocks above, you must ask yourself whether you really want to pursue this specific idea. In other words, have you got the motivation to achieve success with this idea? Think of ways to change the question marks (?) to ticks (✓) and how, for example, you can justify the ticks (✓) to your bank manager.

2. IS THERE A MARKET FOR YOUR IDEA?

☐ Do you know who your consumers will be?

☐ Will they pay you for your product and/or service?

☐ Do you think there are many consumers for your idea? How many (more or less)?

☐ Will people prefer your product and/or service to those of your competitors?

☐ Do you think you will gain more consumers in the future?

☐ What are three advantages you have over your competitors?

1...

2...

3...

☐ Can you prevent other people from copying your idea?

(Adapted from: *The Ideas Generation Workbook* of the Scottish Enterprise Foundation)

If you filled in any question marks (?) in the blocks above, you must ask yourself whether you have a market for this specific idea. How can you change the question marks (?) to ticks (✓), and how can you justify the ticks (✓) to someone like your bank manager?

3. CAN YOU MEET THE NEEDS OF YOUR CONSUMERS?

☐ Do you have, or can you develop, the skills to manufacture your product and/or to provide your service?

☐ Can you provide the quantity and quality of products, or give the level of service, that your consumers want?

☐ Do you know how much money you can charge for your product or service? How much?

☐ If you need someone to help you provide your product or service, do you know anyone who will be willing to do it?

☐ Do you know more or less how much money you will need to start your business? How much?

☐ Do you know how much money you will need in the first year to run your business? How much?

☐ Do you personally have the money to start and run your business? How much do you still need? Where will you get the rest of the money?

If you filled in any question marks (?) in the list, you must ask yourself if you can pursue this idea. Think of ways to turn the question marks (?) into ticks (✓), and how you will, for example, justify the ticks (✓) to a bank manager.

4. CAN YOU GET THE IDEA TO THE CONSUMER?

- ☐ Do you know how your consumer buys this product and/or service?
- ☐ Is there a special magazine, newspaper or journal that your consumers read? What is it?
- ☐ Do you know of any agents or intermediaries who are currently selling to your consumers? Who are they?
- ☐ Do you know of any businesses or organisations who are currently doing business with your consumers? Where are they?
- ☐ Will these businesses or organisations be prepared to promote your idea?
- ☐ Can you get the names and addresses of a large number of potential consumers? About how many?
- ☐ Do you already have various consumers who have indicated that they will buy from you? How many?

(Adapted from: *The Ideas Generation Workbook* of the Scottish Enterprise Foundation)

The question marks (?) in the questionnaire above are not very important. What is important is that there must be many ticks (✓). If you do not have any ticks (✓), or only one or two, you must ask yourself if you should pursue this idea. How can you turn the question marks (?) into ticks (✓), and how can you justify the ticks (✓) to your bank manager, for example?

How do feel about your small business idea, now that you have answered all the above questions? **Complete** the rating scale on the opposite page quickly by circling the number that represents your choice. *(Idea obtained from the Scottish Enterprise Foundation.)*

☞

☞	LEVEL OF CONVICTION			
	Very high	High	Average	Low
❑ Do you want to do what the idea suggests?	4	3	2	1
❑ Is there a market for your idea?	4	3	2	1
❑ Can you meet your consumers' needs?	4	3	2	1
❑ Can you get the idea to the consumers?	4	3	2	1

By counting the numbers that you circled, you can make the following **deductions** from your results:

5 or less	If you definitely feel that it is not for you, you must start the process of identifying ideas from the beginning.
6 to 12	If you are still undecided, you must go back to your list of small business ideas and consider other options.
12 and above	Your idea is feasible and must be explored further.

If you have found, by means of the results above, that your small business idea is in fact feasible, you can go on to investigate its viability. Since the viability study is very expensive in terms of time and money, it is important that you first do the feasibility study as shown above. In Chapter 4 you will be guided step by step in investigating the viability of a small business idea.

SUMMARY

In this chapter we took the first step in setting up a small business, namely the identification of feasible small business ideas.

A small business idea does not always have to be innovative, but it must stand out from other competitive products or services. This requires that the entrepreneur must be able to act **creatively**. The creative abilities of prospective entrepreneurs can be improved in various ways, such as thinking unconventionally or viewing a matter from another person's perspective.

The **techniques** by which small business ideas can be generated can be divided into five broad approaches: from the skills, expertise and aptitudes of the entrepreneur; from common needs; from existing problems; from everyday activities; and from other sources. These approaches can take place separately or in combination. You might encounter a problem, for example, in a work situation and develop it further by means of the ideas-from-problems technique.

A small business idea must be able to be **defined** in terms of its business activity and consumers before it is evaluated and developed.

By matching the small business ideas with questions on how the prospective entrepreneur feels about the specific idea, its **feasibility** can be determined. Small business ideas must also be **viable** before they can be turned into a small business. The viability of small business ideas is discussed in the next chapter.

SELF-EVALUATION

1. **Name** the two most important components of the planning stage in the setting-up of a business.

    ....

    ....

2. **Explain** how you can improve your creative abilities.

    ....

    ....

    ....

    ....
    ☞

3. **Regard** the concept 'honesty' from the point of view of:
   (a) a business person;
   (b) a parent;
   (c) a student.
   What new ideas do you now have about the concept 'honesty'?

   ....
   ....
   ....

4. **List** the five broad techniques that can be used to find small business ideas.

   ....
   ....
   ....
   ....

5. Suppose you are thinking of installing wooden cupboards, shelves and ceilings in houses. **Explain** how you can use the Yellow Pages to identify small business ideas.

   ....
   ....

6. **Distinguish** between a feasibility study and a viability study.

   ....
   ....
   ....

7. Read the case study below and answer the questions.

CASE STUDY: Betty's touring business

After 10 years of raising children, Betty decides to start her own business. As a result of her husband's position, people from overseas often stay at their house. She and her husband often take their guests to the tourist attractions in their vicinity. As there is no touring agency in their area, she is thinking of arranging tours for overseas tourists. Betty is even considering opening a guesthouse and combining it with the touring business.

(a) Define Betty's small business idea in terms of the business activities that it will perform and the consumers that it will serve.

....

....

....

(b) Use the bow-tie technique to develop Betty's idea further.

IDEA

(c) Which four main questions must Betty ask herself to determine the feasibility of her small business idea?.................................

....

....

....

REFERENCES

Albert, K.J. 1977. *How to Pick the Right Small Business Opportunity.* New York: McGraw-Hill.

Clark, I., Louw, E. & Myburgh, J. 1993. *More Small Business Opportunities in South Africa.* Cape Town: Struik.

Miller, W.C. 1987. *The Creative Edge: Fostering Innovation Where You Work.* New York: Addison-Wesley.

Neethling, K. 1993. *Kreatiwiteit laat jou wondere verrig.* Clubview: Benedic Books.

Richardson, P. & Clarke, L. 1990. *Good Ideas Don't Come Out of the Blue – You Have to Work at Them …* The Scottish Enterprise Foundation for the Training Agency: Crown.

Timmons, J.A. 1985. *New Venture Creation: Entrepreneurship in the 1990's.* Boston: Irwin.

4 THE VIABILITY OF A BUSINESS IDEA

LEARNING OBJECTIVES (OUTCOMES)

After you have studied this chapter, you should be able to perform a viability study for a proposed business idea, to enable you to decide whether you should implement it. To do this, you will have to:

❑ determine whether a need exists for a product;

❑ define the mission and objectives for the enterprise;

❑ determine the market share of the product or service;

❑ determine the income that can be derived from the product or service;

❑ determine the break-even point for the enterprise;

❑ determine whether a sustainable profit can be made;

❑ draw up a cash budget to determine whether the enterprise can service its financial obligations as they occur.

2 INTRODUCTION

By working to the end of Chapter 3, you have completed the first stage in the setting-up of a small business enterprise. You are now ready to start on the second stage, which is the planning stage. (To refresh your memory, take another look at the diagram on page 62.)

Business planning usually has two phases. The first is to establish whether a business idea is viable; this is known as the **viability study**. For an idea to be a viable business idea, you must be able to market the idea and manage your business at a sustainable profit. Only if you find that the idea is viable do you continue to the second phase. During the second phase, you will make a **business plan**, which summarises the conclusions drawn from the viability study. You can then use the business plan to make the business idea known to other people and obtain financing that will enable you to implement the business idea.

An idea is **viable** if you can market the idea and manage a business over time at a **sustainable profit**. An idea is **non-viable** if you cannot manage a business over time at a sustainable profit.

In this chapter, we will do the viability study. Chapter 5 will cover the business plan.

To find out if you are going to make a profit, you need to know what will be your total income from the business, as well as how much it will cost you to generate the income. To determine your total income, you must know how many products you are going to sell and at what price.

To find out how many products you will sell and at what price, you need to do some market research. The outcome of the market research must provide the answers to the following questions:

- ❑ Is there a need for my product or service? (**Need analysis**)
- ❑ Who exactly is going to buy my product or service? (**Customer profile/characteristics**)
- ❑ How many products can I sell or clients can I service? (**Market share**)
- ❑ What price can I charge for the product or service? (**Price analysis**) ☞

☞ You will also need to answer the following questions:
- ❑ How many products must I sell or clients must I service to show a profit?
- ❑ Will I have the cash flow to run my business?

After you have done the need analysis and customer profile, you will be able to decide what you can achieve with your enterprise. You must then define the mission and objectives of your enterprise before continuing with the rest of your market research.

THE NEEDS AND CHARACTERISTICS OF CONSUMERS

The very first step in any viability study is to establish who your customers are and what their needs are. The key to success is to deliver what your customers want to buy, and not just what you want to sell.

In Chapter 2 we explained that people buy in order to satisfy a need. This concept of buying to satisfy a need is not simple. On the one hand, a need can be very strongly felt but not easily defined. On the other hand, there can be various options for satisfying that need. There is generally a distinct difference between the **physical product** that consumers buy and the **image** consumers have of the product. When you are about to provide a product or service to the market, you must determine which need that product or service will satisfy.

Take the example of canned fruit in Chapter 2. Canned fruit can satisfy a range of needs, from simple to complex: it can be a sweet snack, quick and easy dessert or even a status symbol (in the case of luxury items such as Jaque's Treats).

The need of your market (consumers) is the basis of your marketing strategy. It is one thing to determine what the consumers want, but it is another matter altogether to meet that need profitably. Therefore first you must work out how you can provide the right product or service at the right price so that you can still make a profit. **You should never enter a market if you cannot do it profitably, no matter how great the need of the consumers.**

To establish if there is a need for a product or service, an entrepreneur can use a method like the following.

(a) List the features of the product/service. It is important to list all the features, as people buy products or sevices to meet various needs. Examples of special features are:
- ❑ The fruit is preserved in an unusual tangy syrup.
- ❑ It is bottled in decorative glass bottles.
- ❑ Exotic tropical fruits are used.

(b) Determine what each feature can mean to the client. Do this by using the phrase *this means that* ... for each feature. Fill in the blanks in the examples that follow.

The use of an unusual tangy syrup means that ...
- ❑ the fruit will have a special taste;
- ❑ it can be used as a dessert;
- ❑ it can be used with other dishes;
- ❑ it can be served to smart guests;
- ❑ it can be used for special occasions;
- ❑ it can be bought as a present.

The use of decorative glass bottles means that ...
- ❑ it can be used as a decorating feature in the kitchen or dining room;
- ❑ it can be bought as a present;
- ❑ it can be bought to decorate the kitchen or dining room;
- ❑ ....
- ❑ ....

The use of exotic tropical fruit means that ...
- ❑ ....
- ❑ ....
- ❑ .... ☞

(c) Determine who occupies the market, and who are the industry leaders, suppliers and other experts on this product or service. Look for information in magazines, newspapers and government documents. Ask other people for their opinion. Test the features of your product on these people (**test marketing**). This will tell you whether there is a need for the product. These tests can also give you valuable additional information on needs in the market to which you can adapt your product or service.

In Jaque's case study, she can consult culinary experts, restaurants, home industries, delicatessens, etc. to see what is the exact need in the market for her specific product.

(d) Identify the possible consumers and organise them into buzz groups. A buzz group is a group of people who meet and exchange ideas. Topics for discussion could include the following:
❑ What are the strong and weak points of the product or service?
❑ What are the characteristics of the consumers who will buy the specific product or service?
   - Where do the consumers live?
   - What are their ages?
   - What do they earn?
   - What is their level of training?
   - What do they do in their leisure time?
   - What is their lifestyle?
   - How much will potential consumers spend on the product or service?
   - How will price changes affect the consumer?
   - Who in the household decides to buy the product or service?
   - How is the product or service used?
   - When will the product or service be used?
   - Why will the customer buy the specific product or service and not a similar product or service?

(e) Now use the information obtained and draw up a final list of:
❑ the features of your product or service;
❑ the needs of the consumers that the product or service will meet;
❑ a profile of your consumers;
❑ the potential number of consumers.

With this information at your disposal, you can now determine what kind of enterprise you wish to start. You can thus **define** your enterprise and **determine your objectives**.

1. Suppose you walk into a hardware store and see a concrete drill. Write down five needs that the drill possibly meets.

   ....
   ....
   ....
   ....
   ....

2. You have bought the book *Entrepreneurship and How to Establish Your Own Business*. Write down the needs that you wanted to satisfy by buying this book.

   ....
   ....

3. Write down several items of your own choosing and see what needs they really meet.

   ....
   ....
   ....
   ....

4. Betty wants to open a guesthouse and arrange tours for overseas tourists.
   ❑ Write down two sources that Betty can consult to find out more about the industry. ....
   ....
   ....

   ❑ List four features of the service she is going to offer. ....
   ....
   ....
   ....
   ....

   ❑ Explain how Betty can determine which consumer needs her product will satisfy. ....
   ....
   ....
   ....

4 THE MISSION AND OBJECTIVES OF THE ENTERPRISE

In Chapter 2, the mission and objectives of the enterprise were broadly described as 'what you want to achieve ... and how you will achieve it'. In this section we will look at the mission and objectives in a lot more detail.

By this time you should know what kind of enterprise you want to run. An important task that you must now fulfil is to define the mission of your enterprise so that you know exactly what you intend to do with your enterprise. This is an important task and needs some thought.

It is usual to define an enterprise according to **the product or service** that you wish to sell, as well as the **consumer profile**. The definition must not be too narrow or too broad. If it is too narrow, it might exclude possible opportunities, but a definition that is too general can cause a lack of enterprise focus. The following questions will help you define your enterprise:

❑ Who are the consumers of the enterprise?
❑ Which needs of the consumers will the enterprise satisfy?
❑ How will the enterprise satisfy the needs of the consumers?

By following the steps outlined in the previous section of this chapter, you have already collected the information to answer the above questions. You can now proceed to define the mission of the enterprise.

We can use the case study of Jaque's Treats to draw up a mission statement for her enterprise.

MISSION FOR THE ENTERPRISE: JAQUE'S TREATS

First answer the following three questions:

1. Who are the consumers of Jaque's Treats?
❑ Individuals who enjoy entertaining and who would like to serve something special.
❑ Individuals who want to impress other people with their skill at cooking.
❑ Individuals who do not mind paying a high price for an exceptional product. ☞

❏ Individuals who can afford something special on a regular basis.
❏ Individuals who want to give somebody a special gift.

2. Which needs of consumers will be satisfied?
❏ To be regarded as a super hostess/host in an elite community.
❏ To have the pleasure of enjoying an expensive choice product on a regular basis.
❏ To be regarded as someone who gives exceptional and choice gifts.

3. How will consumers' needs be satisfied?
❏ Provide choice-grade canned litchis and mangoes in a variety of highly tangy spiced syrups.
❏ Pack the fruit very attractively and colourfully in exceptional decorative bottles.
❏ Provide a special recipe and alternative serving suggestions for each bottle of fruit.

A mission for this enterprise could be:
Jaque's Treats will preserve high-quality fruits in tangy syrups and package and sell them very attractively in decorative glass bottles so as to satisfy individuals' sophisticated and exclusive tastes.

Now that you know what kind of enterprise you want to start, you can define objectives for the enterprise. The objectives must be **measurable and attainable** milestones which do not **change easily in the short term**. (Objectives are also discussed in Chapter 2, section 5.)

An example of an **objective** could be to show a 10% return on capital within the first two years of the enterprise's existence.

Objectives must be set so that you have something to measure progress against. Objectives usually change together with a changing business environment. A good objective must meet the following criteria: it must be **quantifiable, understandable, realistic, time-specific, flexible and consistent**.

Now you know exactly what your enterprise will and will not do. This will help you calculate your market share, so that you can work out if your product or service can be marketed profitably. It is very important that you make **realistic predictions**. Whatever you do, do not be too optimistic in your predictions. It does not help to mislead yourself. If you are too optimistic, it can lead to failure.

1. Well-defined objectives meet at least six criteria. Write down the six criteria.

   ....
   ....
   ....
   ....
   ....
   ....

2. Answer the following questions and then write down a mission statement for Betty's guesthouse.

   ❑ Who are the consumers of the service Betty will provide?

   ....

   ❑ Which needs of her consumers will her product satisfy?

   ....
   ....

   ❑ How will the needs be satisfied?

   ....
   ....

   ❑ What would be a mission statement for Betty's guesthouse and touring business?

   ....
   ....
   ....
   ....

3. Write down three objectives for Betty's guesthouse and touring business. Make sure that your objectives reflect the criteria for a well-defined objective.

   ....
   ....
   ....

5 CALCULATE THE EXPECTED MARKET SHARE

It is essential to calculate your expected market share as accurately as possible, as this will give you the information you need to calculate your potential income. Your potential income must be calculated as accurately as possible, otherwise you will not really be able to determine whether your business idea will be profitable.

To calculate your expected market share, you start by calculating the **total market potential** for your product. Then you must consider what portion of this market is occupied by your competitors and what portion you can address. The section that you can serve is known as your **target market**. Lastly, you must establish what your **expected market share** will be.

5.1 Potential market

It is not easy to analyse a potential market. Most entrepreneurs work with **unquantified information** and must make many **assumptions**. However, when you identified the need that exists for your product, you collected much of the information needed to segment your market.

When analysing the market, you must divide it into the various market segments.

A market can, for example, be segmented geographically and demographically, and in terms of the lifestyle and buying patterns of consumers.

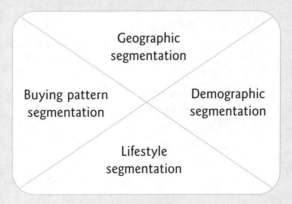

MARKET SEGMENTATION

Here are some examples of questions that will help you segment your market:

QUESTIONS	ANSWERS	FILL IN THE ANSWERS FOR BETTY'S GUEST-HOUSE AND TOURING SERVICE
GEOGRAPHIC SEGMENTATION ❑ Where do the consumers of your product live? Or, where is there a concentration of these consumers?	❑ Gauteng area.	
❑ Where do the consumers work and how do they travel to work?	❑ Work in Pretoria and Johannes-burg and travel to work by car.	
❑ Where do your consumers spend their leisure time?	❑ At home, with friends and family.	
DEMOGRAPHIC SEGMENTATION ❑ What is the nationality, race and religion of the consumers?	❑ Chiefly South Africans, of all races and religions.	
❑ What is the consumer's average age, sex and social class?	❑ Thirty years, male or female and well-off.	
❑ What is the consumer's level of education, occupation and income?	❑ High level of education, mainly professional, income about R150 000 plus a year.	☞

❏ What is the average size of the consumer's household?	❏ Five members.	
LIFESTYLE SEGMENTATION		
❏ How do consumers spend their free time?	❏ Entertaining.	
❏ How do consumers entertain?	❏ Formal dinners and informal barbecues.	
❏ What do they spend money on?	❏ Clothes, entertaining, holidays.	
❏ What hobbies do the consumers have?	❏ Play golf, entertain go to gym regularly.	
BUYING PATTERN SEGMENTATION		
❏ When do the consumers buy the product or service?	❏ At any time during the year.	
❏ What benefit do the consumers want from the product or service?	❏ Status.	
❏ How often do consumers buy the product or service?	❏ Weekly.	
❏ Who decides to buy the product or service?	❏ The hostess/host.	

Use the third column to analyse the potential market for Betty's guesthouse and touring service.

After you have done the market segmentation, examine each segment again in terms of:

☐ **Measurability**: Can you determine the number of consumers in the segment?

☐ **Profitability**: Is the consumer able to pay a price for your product that will enable you to make a profit?

☐ **Accessibility**: Will you be able to reach the consumers? Stiff competition between enterprises often makes it difficult for new arrivals to reach consumers.

1. You want to open a fish franchise in your neighbourhood. Segment your market and analyse the potential market.

   ....
   ....
   ....
   ....
   ....
   ....
   ....
   ....

2. Will you enter the market? State the reasons for your answer.

   ....
   ....
   ....
   ....

5.2 The target market

The target market is that portion of the market that you can reach with your product or service.

To determine your target market, you must find out what part of the total potential market is served by **your competitors**. You can do this by making a list of your competitors and then identifying which market segment is their target market.

TOTAL MARKET POTENTIAL	–	MARKET SHARE OF COMPETITORS	=	TARGET MARKET

To identify which market segment is their target market, you need to answer the following questions about your competitors:

❑ Who are your closest competitors?
❑ What are the strengths and weaknesses of your strongest competitors?
❑ How do their enterprises compare with yours? How do they differ and how are they similar? (For example, size, product, manufacture, situation.)
❑ Who are their consumers?
❑ Why would a consumer prefer your competitor's product or service to yours?
❑ What is their sales volume in the product or service that you also wish to sell?
❑ What is their price structure? How does it compare with yours? (For example, are their products or services cheaper or more expensive?)
❑ What is each competitor's market share? (For example, 20% belongs to competitor 'A' and 30% to competitor 'B'.)
❑ Is their target share growing or shrinking?
❑ How do they market their products or services?
❑ What image does the enterprise and its product or service project?
❑ How is the product or service distributed? (For example, only available from supermarkets and garages.)
❑ What is the possibility that they can copy your product or service?

☞

❏ Are there potential competitors who have not yet entered the market, but could do so in the near future?

❏ How saturated is the market? Is there sufficient opportunity for your enterprise to make it worth entering the market?

After analysing your competitors, you must decide **how well you can compete with them**. The best way to do this is to determine your enterprise's **strengths and weaknesses**, and identify the **opportunities and threats** that exist in the market.

You want to calculate the target market for the fish franchise that you plan to open in your neighbourhood.

❏ First determine the target market of your competitors by answering the above questions about your competitors.

....

....

....

....

....

....

....

....

....

....

....

....

....

....

....

❏ Then define your own target markets.

....

....

....

5.3 Expected market share

Sometimes an enterprise cannot satisfy the potential demand for a product or service as the **enterprise's capacity** restricts the number of products that can be provided. When the **economy** is in decline, consumers are not able to satisfy their need for the product, because they do not have the necessary money/credit to buy it. These kinds of restrictions indicate that an enterprise must determine what its market share must be in certain circumstances.

> The expected market share is that part of the target that an enterprise will be able to serve on the basis of its production capacity and the state of the economy.

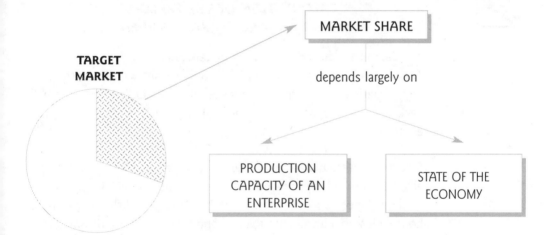

It is very important to calculate the expected market share as accurately as possible, as it has a direct influence on the calculation of your income.

As you know, an enterprise operates under uncertain conditions. You will never know exactly what your market share will be. To reduce the risk, you should calculate the **expected market share for different scenarios**:

❑ an extremely prosperous scenario;
❑ a most probable scenario;
❑ a very weak scenario.

Calculate the **profit** for each scenario and judge from that whether it is worth going ahead with the business idea and starting an enterprise. This kind of calculation is also **imperative** if you intend to obtain financing from a source like a bank.

So:

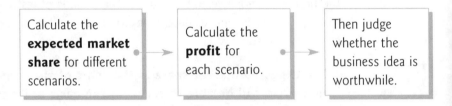

| Calculate the **expected market share** for different scenarios. | → | Calculate the **profit** for each scenario. | → | Then judge whether the business idea is worthwhile. |

CALCULATION OF THE EXPECTED MARKET SHARE OF JAQUE'S TREATS

1. Calculate the total market potential

According to the mission of Jaque's enterprise, she will concentrate on high-quality preserved fruit in very special spicy sauces, which she will package very expensively and decoratively for a sophisticated and exclusive market.

Statistical research has shown her that there are 500 000 extremely affluent and sophisticated households in South Africa. These households are mostly in the cities. She has also established that these households do a lot of entertaining, and that they serve dessert every day. Jaque's preserved fruit could be served as a dessert or as an ingredient in exotic dishes.

Her market research indicates that she could sell at least 1 000 000 bottles of fruit each month. Jaque's potential market therefore seems to be 1 000 000 bottles of fruit a month. But this is merely a general assessment of the market potential. Now Jaque will have to determine what her target market will be.

2. Calculate the target market

Jaque must now determine how much of this potential market is already served by her competitors. Her original research showed that

☞

there are five competitors in the market. They preserve fruit, but only in ordinary sugar syrup. Not one of them packs the fruit in bottles. These competitors produce about 1 000 000 cans of fruit a month. However, their production is not aimed only at the exotic market. They serve all socio-economic levels. Over and above these five large competitors, there are numerous smaller home industries that also preserve fruit. These smaller enterprises usually pack the fruit in glass bottles.

Jaque has calculated that all the competitors combined serve about 800 000 of the potential market of 1 000 000. The lower socio-economic levels buy the rest of their production. Her target market is thus about 200 000 monthly.

3. Calculate the expected market share

The current availability of production factors (money, labour and raw material) limit Jaque's production to 3 000 bottles a month. Her expected market share therefore cannot be more than 3 000 bottles a month. As her enterprise grows and she obtains more capital, she will be able to increase her production capacity and enlarge her expected market share.

As Jaque cannot be certain of the state of the economy, she has decided to draw up scenarios for very sound, average and poor economic conditions. When the economy is very sound, she expects to sell her full production of 3 000 bottles; when it is average, 2 000; and when it is poor, 1 000 bottles.

For more information on this topic, consult Machado, R. and Cassim, S. *Marketing Management for Small Business* (Juta).

Now that you have calculated the expected market share, you can calculate the income from the business idea.

CALCULATE THE INCOME

To calculate the income, you must first calculate the selling price of your product or service. To do this, you must calculate all the costs incurred in manufacturing and selling a product. You must know what the **total cost**

per unit (cost price) will be before you calculate the selling price of your product. **The selling price must at least cover all the costs.** If this is not the case, your enterprise will show a loss from the start. (Please note: a 'unit' can refer either to one product that we manufacture, or one that we buy and sell or one hour that a service enterprise charges for services rendered; for example, the rate per hour you pay the garage for servicing your car.)

The next step in calculating the selling price is to add **a percentage profit to the cost price** (cost price + profit = selling price). If you add a mark-up (a percentage profit to the cost price) of, say, 40% and the cost price of the product is R10, the product will sell at 140/100 x R10 = R14,00.

To calculate the selling price by adding a percentage profit to the cost price (mark-up), you must add the percentage mark-up to 100 and then divide it by 100. You then multiply the answer by the cost price of the product.

❑ If you have a 40% mark-up and the cost price of the product is R10, the selling price will be:

40 + 100 = 140

$$\frac{140}{100} = 1,40$$

1,40 x 10 = R14,00 (selling price)

❑ If you have a 60% mark-up and the cost price of the product is R20, the selling price will be:

60 + 100 = 160

$$\frac{160}{100} = 1,6$$

1,6 x 20 = R32 (selling price)

You will have to take the selling price of your competitors into account. You cannot really charge more for your product than your competitors, or you will possibly price yourself out of the market. If your competitor's price is R15 and yours is R14 and you both offer the same benefits to your consumer, your product ought to sell well. But if your competitor's price is R13, then their product or service should sell better.

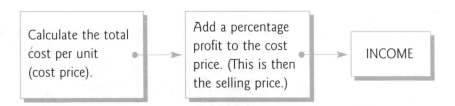

1. Suppose it costs R20 to make a toy horse. At what price should you sell it to make a profit of 40%?

   ....

2. How would it affect your enterprise if two competitors sell their toy horses at:

   (a) R25 each   (a) ....

   (b) R30 each?   (b) ....

6.1 Calculating the total costs per unit of the product (cost price of the product)

When calculating the cost price it is important to classify the costs as:
- ❏ **variable** and **fixed** costs;
- ❏ **direct** and **indirect** costs.

❏ **Variable costs are costs that are fixed per unit, but variable in total.** This means that the costs rise in direct relation to the number of units manufactured (see graph below). For example, if the raw materials in a product cost R1, and 10 products are manufactured, the total variable costs are R10. If 20 products are manufactured, the total variable cost is R20, but it is still R1 for one product.

We can show variable costs on a graph as follows:

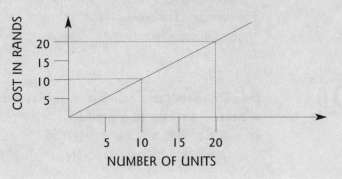

❑ **Fixed costs are the costs that are fixed in total, but variable per unit**. Look at the following graph. The rent on a factory is R100 (point A), but per product it is R10. If 20 products are manufactured, the total fixed cost is still R100 (point B), but per product it is R5.

We can show fixed costs on a graph as follows:

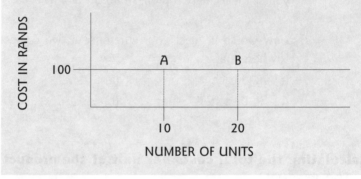

 The total cost of a product is equal to the fixed costs plus the variable costs.

FIXED COSTS + VARIABLE COSTS = TOTAL COSTS

 Direct costs are costs that can be allocated directly to the product at manufacturing of the product.
Examples of direct costs are the raw materials that are used for the manufacture of a product and wages of labourers who are directly involved in manufacturing the product.

 Indirect costs (also called overheads) are costs that cannot be allocated directly to a product.
Examples of these costs are rent on the factory, electricity, water, depreciation and indirect wages (like the salary of the owner).

1.1 Write down the definition of the following costs:

Variable costs ....

....

Fixed costs ....

....

Direct costs ....

....

Indirect costs ....

....

1.2 Give two examples for each of these costs for a fish franchise:

....

....

....

....

....

....

....

2. Why do you think it is necessary to classify costs in this way?

....

....

3. Answer the following questions and give a reason for each answer:

(a) Can a variable cost be a direct cost?

....

(b) Can a variable cost be an indirect cost?

....

(c) Can an indirect cost be a fixed cost?

....

The way you calculate the costs of a product will depend on the kind of enterprise you are operating. **The three main types of enterprises are:**

❏ manufacturing enterprises;
❏ service enterprises;
❏ business (commercial) enterprises.

(a) Calculate the total costs per unit of a product for a manufacturing enterprise

The total costs of a product in a manufacturing enterprise consist of **manufacturing costs plus commercial costs**.

Manufacturing costs consist of **direct labour** costs (the wages of the factory workers), **direct material costs** (the costs of raw materials like sugar or wood) and **manufacturing overhead costs (indirect costs)**.

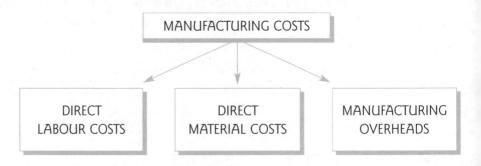

Commercial overhead costs consist of **administrative overheads** and **marketing overheads**.

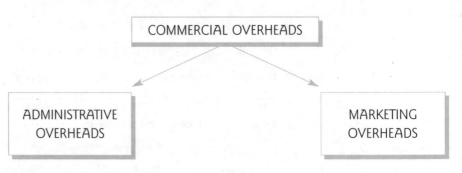

Administrative overhead costs are all costs related to the administration of the enterprise functions, such as human resources, finance and management. **Marketing costs** are all the costs incurred in marketing a product.

The following steps can be taken to calculate the total costs of one unit of a product.

❑ Calculate the **direct costs of the materials** that are used to manufacture one unit of a product. In Jaque's case, this means calculating the cost of the fruit, sugar, herbs and bottle for one bottle of preserved fruit. Suppose it is R2.

❑ Calculate the **direct labour costs** needed to manufacture one unit of a product. Suppose it is R3 in Jaque's case.

❑ Calculate the **indirect costs** per unit of the product. (Add the manufacturing overheads, marketing overheads and administrative overheads together and divide this total by the number of products that were manufactured in the same period the costs were incurred; for example, one month.) Suppose it is R5.

❑ Add the costs together to get the total costs per unit. In our example the figure is R10. (Direct costs of materials = R2 + Direct labour costs = R3 + Indirect costs = R5.)

So:

COSTS PER UNIT FOR A MANUFACTURING ENTERPRISE

DIRECT COSTS OF MATERIALS		DIRECT LABOUR COSTS		INDIRECT COSTS		TOTAL COSTS
	+		+		=	

(b) Calculate the total costs per hour for a service enterprise

In a service enterprise, the product that is for sale is knowledge and skill. A repair service is a good example of a service enterprise. In this kind of enterprise, the entrepreneur must calculate how much it costs per hour to devote her/his attention to a matter.

The following steps can be taken to calculate the total costs of one unit of a product:

❑ **Calculate the number of business hours per month.** Business hours are the hours during which the enterprise conducts business, for example daily from 8:00 to 17:00 (in other

☞

117

words, 9 hours a day). Six days a week × 9 hours = 54 hours a week × 52 weeks = 2 808 hours a year/12 months = 234 hours a month.

❑ **Calculate the cost per hour**. Calculate the total expenses for a month, for example rent on the building, salaries, rental on office equipment, etc. Suppose it is R10 000 a month. Divide the total costs by the number of working hours per month: R10 000/234 hours = R42,73 an hour. This means that you cannot charge less than R42,73 an hour for your services.

So:

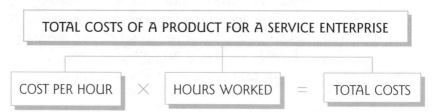

TOTAL COSTS OF A PRODUCT FOR A SERVICE ENTERPRISE

| COST PER HOUR | × | HOURS WORKED | = | TOTAL COSTS |

(c) Calculate the total costs per product for a commercial enterprise
A commercial enterprise does not manufacture products. It buys finished products and then sells them again at a higher price.

The total costs for a product in a commercial enterprise are made up of the purchasing costs of the product that is to be sold (this is called the cost of sales) plus the commercial overhead costs.

❑ **Calculate the costs of sales of one product** for a commercial enterprise (for example, a women's clothing store).
Stock at the beginning of a month

10 dresses @ R100 per dress	R1 000
Plus: Purchase of dresses during the month	
(10 dresses @ R110 per dress)	R1 100
	R2 100
Minus stock at the end of the month	
(5 dresses @ R100 per dress)	R 500
Cost of sales (15 dresses) (5 × R100 + 10 × R110)	R1 600
Cost of sales per dress (R1 600/15)	R 107

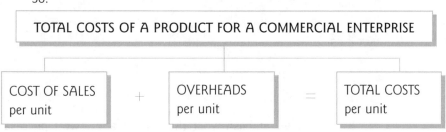

❏ **Calculate the contribution of the overheads.** Suppose the administrative and marketing overheads are R1 000. The overheads per unit sold are R1 000/15 = R67.

❏ The total costs per unit = Cost of sales per unit + overheads per unit = R107 + R67 = R174.

So:

TOTAL COSTS OF A PRODUCT FOR A COMMERCIAL ENTERPRISE

COST OF SALES per unit	+	OVERHEADS per unit	=	TOTAL COSTS per unit

6.2 Calculate the selling price

The price you can charge for your product or service is directly influenced by the price that your **competitors** charge for the same kind of product or service. If your product or service is much more expensive than that of your competitors, you will lose customers. Your product or service can only be more expensive than that of your competitors if you offer more benefits to your consumers than your competitors do.

To determine what you can charge for your product, you must list your products and then establish what your competitors charge for similar products. Then list your competitors' strengths and weaknesses. Also list your own enterprise's strengths and weaknesses and compare them with those of your competitors.

YOUR OWN ENTERPRISE	COMPETITOR'S ENTERPRISE
List of products and prices	List of products and prices
1. .... R	1. .... R ....
2. .... R	2. .... R ....
3. .... R	3. .... R ....

☞

Strengths	Strengths
1.	1. ....
2.	2. ....
3.	3. ....
Weaknesses	Weaknesses
1.	1. ....
2.	2. ....
3.	3. ....

You can now establish what the highest and lowest prices are and also what price tendencies (the prices charged for the product or service in general) apply to the product or service. If an enterprise has exceptional strengths, this can justify high prices. The converse is also true: if the enterprise has many weaknesses it will be obliged to charge lower prices than its competitors.

After you have made the comparison, you can decide what you can charge for your products or services. Remember that you may never charge less than the total cost of a product or service.

Having established the **selling price** of your product, you can now **calculate the income from the sale of the product**.

1. How do the prices of competitor's products influence the price you can charge for a similar product?

   ....

   ....

   ....

2. Is it necessary to take note of the prices that competitors charge for similar products? Give reasons for your answers.

   ....

   ....

   ....

7 CALCULATE THE EXPECTED NET PROFIT

You have now reached the point where you can test the **viability** of your business idea. To be viable, the business idea must be **profitable**. You calculate your profit by deducting your total expenses from your total income. If the income exceeds the expenses, you are making a **profit**. If, on the other hand, your expenses exceed your income, you are making a **loss**.

So:

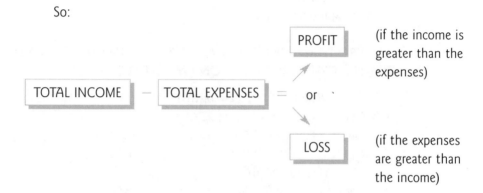

			PROFIT	(if the income is greater than the expenses)
TOTAL INCOME	– TOTAL EXPENSES	= or		
			LOSS	(if the expenses are greater than the income)

The net profit is calculated by drawing up a pro forma income statement.

A pro forma income statement is an income statement that is drawn up by using estimated figures.

Usually you calculate the net profit for the various scenarios that you determined (see section 5.3).

We will learn more about calculating the net profit by looking again at our case study.

CALCULATE THE NET PROFIT OF JAQUE'S TREATS

Jaque's Treats can sell at least 2 000 bottles of preserved fruit a month for at least R15 a bottle.

The monthly expenses of Jaque's Treats are the following:
❑ Direct materials – R4 000 (fruit, sugar, bottles, etc.).
❑ Rent on the factory – R1 500.

- Water and electricity for the factory – R500.
- Water and electricity for the office – R100.
- Marketing costs – R1 000.
- Depreciation on equipment – R800.
- Delivery costs – R1 500.
- Salary to the owner (Jaque) for managing the enterprise – R4 000.
- Administrative salaries – R2 000.
- Direct wages – R6 000.
- Telephone – R300.
- Stationery – R100.

PRO FORMA INCOME STATEMENT FOR JAQUE'S TREATS FOR THE FIRST YEAR OF OPERATION (WORST SCENARIO)

Sales (2 000 x R15 x 12 months)		R360 000
Less: Cost of sales		R153 600
Direct materials (R4 000 x 12)	R48 000	
Direct labour (R6 000 x 12)	R72 000	
Manufacturing overheads:		
Rent on factory (R1 500 x 12)	R18 000	
Water and electricity (R500 x 12)	R6 000	
Depreciation on equipment	R9 600	
GROSS INCOME		R206 400
Less: Expenses		R108 000
Marketing costs (R1 000 x 12)	R12 000	
Delivery costs (R1 500 x 12)	R18 000	
Salary of owner (R4 000 x 12)	R48 000	
Administrative salaries (R2 000 x 12)	R24 000	
Telephone (R300 x 12)	R3 600	
Stationery (R100 x 12)	R1 200	
Water and electricity	R1 200	
NET PROFIT		R98 400

According to the calculations, Jaque's Treats shows a small profit at the end of the year. She should now calculate how many bottles of preserved fruit she will have to sell before she breaks even, that is, where she makes no profit and also no loss. (This is known as the calculation of the **break-even point**.)

1. What do you have to calculate to test the viability of your business idea?

   ....

2. How do you calculate profit?

   ....

3. Draw up a pro forma income statement for your own business idea and establish whether your business idea is viable.

   ....
   ....
   ....
   ....
   ....
   ....
   ....
   ....
   ....

CALCULATE THE BREAK-EVEN POINT

Even if you are making a profit according to your pro forma income statement, it is still very good to calculate how much worse your business can do without showing a loss. To do this, you must calculate the break-even point.

The break-even point in units can be defined as the number of units that must be sold for the income and expenses to be equal, that is, where the net profit is equal to R0.

The break-even point in units can be calculated using the following formula:

$$\text{Units} = \frac{\text{Fixed Costs}}{\text{Price per unit} - \text{Variable costs per unit}}$$

We will calculate the break-even point by using an example.

CALCULATE THE BREAK-EVEN POINT FOR JAQUE'S TREATS IN UNITS

Use Jaque's Treats' pro forma income statement and calculate the fixed and variable costs. (You can refer to section 6.1 to remind yourself of the differences between variable and fixed costs.)

Variable costs		**R144 000**
Direct materials	R48 000	
Direct labour	R72 000	
Water and electricity	R6 000	
Delivery costs	R18 000	

Fixed costs		**R117 600**
Rent on factory	R18 000	
Depreciation of equipment	R9 600	
Marketing costs	R12 000	
Salary of owner	R48 000	
Administrative salaries	R24 000	
Telephone	R3 600	
Stationery	R1 200	
Water and electricity (office)	R1 200	

$$\text{Units} = \frac{\text{Fixed Costs}}{\text{Price per unit} - \text{Variable costs per unit}}$$

$$\text{Units} = \frac{\text{R117 600}}{\text{R15} - (\text{R144 000}/24\ 000\ \text{units})}$$

$$= \frac{\text{R117 600}}{\text{R15} - \text{R6}}$$

$$= \frac{\text{R117 600}}{\text{R9}}$$

$= 13\ 067$ bottles of preserved fruit.

Jaque now knows that she will show a loss if she sells fewer than 13 067 bottles of preserved fruit a year. She can only enter the market if she is certain to sell more than 13 067 bottles of fruit.

1. Give at least three reasons for the importance of calculating the break-even point.

   (a) ....

   (b) ....

   (c) ....

2. Write down the formula for calculating the break-even point in units.

   ....

3. Paul has a small enterprise selling posters. He has fixed operating costs of R2 500, and the sale price per poster is R10. His variable operating costs per unit are R5 per unit.

   (a) How many units should he sell to break even? *

   ....

   ....

   (b) If Paul sells less than his break-even number of posters, what will happen to his business in the long run?

   ....

   ....

   * Answer: 500 units.

4. Sheryl has a coffee shop. Her fixed costs are R3 000. Her sales price per cup of coffee is R5 and her variable costs per unit are R3.

   (a) What is Sheryl's break-even point? ** ....

   ....

   (b) If Sheryl sells more than 1 500 cups of coffee, what will the effect be on her business? ....

   ....

   ** Answer: 1 500 cups of coffee.

CASH PLANNING: THE CASH BUDGET (CASH FORECAST)

Up to this point, we have stressed the importance of being able to sustain profits over time. It is worth repeating, though. **Do not attempt any business venture if you cannot sustain profits over the long run.**

Unfortunately, making a profit is not enough. While profits are necessary over the long run to sustain a business, it is equally important to have enough cash available to manage the business on a day-to-day basis. You might make a net profit but lack sufficient ready cash (money) to meet expenses as they occur. If this happens, you cannot continue with your business and you will go bankrupt and your enterprise will have to close. When you do not have money to meet expenses as they occur, you are in a situation known as **technical bankruptcy**. If your cash flow is such that you **can meet your expenses** as they occur, you **can stay** in business. If you **cannot meet them** you will not be able to **stay** in business.

To overcome this problem, it is extremely important that you pay close attention to the planning of **actual money flowing in** to your business and **actual money flowing out** of the business. You must make it your first priority to know how much actual money you are going to receive, and on what dates, as well as when you have to pay expenses, and what amounts are involved. A tool you can use to help you with this cash planning is the cash budget.

> **The cash budget is a formal plan for forecasting future receipts and payments of cash.**

The cash budget normally reflects the business cycle of the enterprise. It begins with the purchase of raw materials and ends with the collection of cash from sales. The management of cash would be fairly easy if we bought a product or service for cash and sold it immediately for cash. But it is not that easy. We do not buy everything for cash and we do not sell everything immediately for cash. There are **lag times** between buying raw materials (paying out money), producing the product and selling it (receiving money). It is these **lag times** that can cause **cash-flow problems**. The same situation exists for an enterprise that provides services. The enterprise incurs salaries and other expenses while rendering the service, and typically receives cash at a later date. The cash budget helps you to plan for these lag times, as it shows you when your actual cash inflow and actual cash outflow do not match. You can then arrange for additional financing; for example, a loan from a bank. By knowing when you are going to receive adequate cash to repay the loan, you can also negotiate loan payback terms.

The cash budget is designed to cover a one-year period divided into monthly periods. The key input to the cash budget is the sales forecast.

The **sales forecast** is the prediction of your enterprise's sales over a given period (normally a year). From your projected sales you must estimate the monthly cash flows that will result. On the one hand, you will have cash inflows resulting from sales and, on the other hand, you will have sales-related outlays; for example, the purchasing of stock and payment of rent. From the sales levels you must also predict the level of fixed assets required and the amount of financing needed.

The cash budget is composed of different components. We will explain the cash budget by looking at each component separately.

Format for a cash budget

	Jan	Feb	Mar		Oct	Nov	Dec
Cash receipts							
Less: Cash payments							
Net cash flow							
Add: Beginning cash							
Ending cash (Excess cash or shortfall)							

Cash receipts are all items from which cash inflows result in a given financial period. The most common components of cash receipts are:
❑ **cash sales;**
❑ **cash received from debtors (a debtor is someone who owes you money).**

Peter has a hairdressing salon. He is drawing up a cash budget for January, February and March. He expects sales of R10 000 for January, R12 000 for February and R20 000 for March. He had sales of R30 000 for December and R20 000 for November of the previous year. Traditionally 50% of his sales are in cash and the rest on credit. Half of his debtors to whom he sold on credit will pay within one month, and the other half within two months. No bad debts are expected.

To draw up the cash budget you must **first analyse the sales income** to determine the amount he is going to receive in which month. ☞

Analysis of sales income:

❑ **November sales of R20 000**

Cash sales received in November
- R20 000/2 = R10 000
  Debtors owe R20 000 – R10 000 = R10 000
  Debtors pay 50% of what they owe in December
- R10 000/2 = R5 000
  Debtors pay the rest of what they owe in January (R5 000)

❑ **December sales of R30 000**

Cash sales received in December
- R30 000/2 = R15 000
  Debtors owe R30 000 – R15 000 = R15 000
- Debtors pay what they owe in January
- R15 000/2 = R7 500
  Debtors pay the rest of what they owe in February
- R15 000 – R7 500 = R7 500

❑ **January sales of R10 000**

Cash sales received in January
- R10 000/2 = R5 000
  Debtors owe R10 000 – R5 000 = R5 000
- Debtors pay 50% of what they owe in February
- R5 000/2 = R2 500
  Debtors pay the rest of what they owe in March
- R5 000 – R2 500 = R2 500

❑ **February sales of R12 000**

Cash sales received in February
- R12 000/2 = R6 000
  Debtors owe R12 000 – R6 000 = R6 000
- Debtors pay 50% of what they owe in March
- R6 000/2 = R3 000
  Debtors pay the rest of what they owe in April
- R6 000 – R3 000 = R3 000

❑ **March sales of R20 000**

Cash sales received in March
- R20 000/2 = R10 000
  Debtors owe R20 000 – R10 000 = R10 000
- Debtors pay 50% in April
- R10 000/2 = R5 000
  Debtors pay the rest of what they owe in May
- R10 000 – R5 000 = R5 000

To summarise, the above can be represented as follows:

Sales income

Nov	Dec	Jan	Feb	March	April	May
R20 000	**R30 000**	**R10 000**	**R12 000**	**R20 000**		

The above is for information only and to help you calculate.

R10 000	R5 000	R5 000				
	R15 000	R7 500	R7 500			
		R5 000	R2 500	R2 500		
			R6 000	R3 000	R3 000	
				R10 000	R5 000	R5 000
		R17 500	R16 000	R15 500	R8 000	R5 000

	Jan	Feb	Mar
Forecast sales	**R10 000**	**R12 000**	**R20 000**

The above is for information only and to help you calculate.

	Jan	Feb	Mar
Cash Sales	R5 000	R6 000	R10 000
Collections from debtors:			
Lagged one month (50%)	R7 500	R2 500	R3 000
Lagged two months (50%)	R5 000	R7 500	R2 500
Total cash receipts	R17 500	R16 000	R15 500

Cash payments

Cash payments include all payments made within the specific period of the cash budget. Examples of cash payments are:
❑ **cash purchases;**
❑ **payments to creditors (people you owe money to);**
❑ **rent or lease payments;**

☞

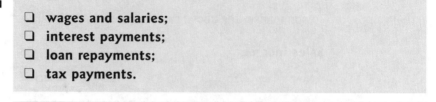

- ❏ **wages and salaries;**
- ❏ **interest payments;**
- ❏ **loan repayments;**
- ❏ **tax payments.**

Please note that only actual cash payments are included in the cash budget.

The following expenses must be paid by Peter's Hair Salon:
- ❏ Purchases for Peter's Hair Salon are 20% of the previous month's sales. Fifty per cent of the purchases are made for cash and the rest is paid to the suppliers in the following month. (Suppliers, other people or institutions you owe money to are your creditors.) R2 000 must be paid to creditors in January.
- ❏ Rent of R2 000 a month must be paid.
- ❏ Salaries of R4 000 a month must be paid.
- ❏ Hairdressers' commission of 10% of previous month's sales.
- ❏ A monthly instalment of R1 000 for redemption of a loan.
- ❏ In March a loan of R8 000 must be redeemed.

Schedule of projected cash payments for Peter's Hair Salon

	Dec	Jan	Feb	March
Purchases	**R4 000**	**R6 000**	**R2 000**	**R2 400**

The above is for information only and to help you calculate.

	Dec	Jan	Feb	March
Cash purchases	R2 000	R3 000	R1 000	R1 200
Creditors: Lag one month		R2 000	R3 000	R1 000
Rent		R2 000	R2 000	R2 000
Salaries		R4 000	R4 000	R4 000
Commission		R3 000	R1 000	R1 200
Loan repayment		R1 000	R1 000	R1 000
Loan redemption				R8 000
Total cash payments		R15 000	R12 000	R18 400

Purchases: 20% of previous month's sales
- Purchases for January = Sales for December × 20/100
  R30 000 × 20/100 = R6 000
  Cash purchases = R6 000/2 = R3 000
  Purchases on credit (Creditors' lag one month) = R6 000/2
  = R3 000 (paid in February)

- Purchases for February = Sales for January × 20/100
  R10 000 × 20/100 = R2 000
  Cash purchases = R2 000/2 = R1 000
  Purchases on credit (Creditors' lag one month) = R2 000/2
  = R1 000 (paid in March)

- Purchases for March = Sales for February × 20/100
  R12 000 × 20/100 = R2 400
  Cash purchases = R2 400/2 = R1 200
  Purchases on credit (Creditors' lag one month) = R2 400/2
  = R1 200 (paid in April)

Commission
- Commission for January = Sales for December × 10/100
  R30 000 × 10/100 = R3 000
- Commission for February = Sales for January × 10/100
  R10 000 × 10/100 = R1 000
- Commission for March = Sales for February × 10/100
  R12 000 × 10/100 = R1 200

Net cash flow

You can find the net cash flow by subtracting the cash payments from the cash receipts in each period.

Net cash flow schedule

	Jan	Feb	March
Total cash receipts	R17 500	R16 000	R15 500
Total cash payments	R15 000	R12 000	R18 400
Net cash flow per month	R2 500	R4 000	(R2 900)

January and February each have a positive net cash flow, but March has a negative cash flow (Peter needs more money than he made).

Ending cash flow

> **The ending cash flow is the net cash flow plus the beginning cash flow.**
>
> **The beginning cash flow of a month is the ending cash flow from the previous month.**

Peter informs us that he had an ending cash flow of R3 000 for December. Calculate the ending cash flow for January, February and March.

	Jan	Feb	March
Net cash flow	R2 500	R4 000	(R2 900)
+ Beginning cash flow	R3 000	R5 500	R9 500
= Ending cash flow	R5 500	R9 500	R16 600

We can now do the cash budget for Peter's Hair Salon.

Cash Budget for Peter's Hair Salon			
	Jan	Feb	March
Total cash receipts	R17 500	R16 000	R15 500
− Total cash payments	R15 000	R12 000	R18 400
= Net cash flow	R2 500	R4 000	(R2 900)
+ Beginning cash flow	R3 000	R5 500	R9 500
= Ending cash	R5 500	R9 500	R6 600

For further information about the cash budget, consult Kritzinger A.A.C. and Fourie J.C.W., *Basic Principles of Financial Management for a Small Business* (Juta).

From the above you can see how a cash budget enables you to forecast your short-term cash requirements.

If you are working on a very tight budget it is advisable that you shorten the time span of the cash budget so that you can monitor your cash flows more frequently than on a monthly basis. Depending on how tight your budget is, you can either work with a weekly or a daily budget. The greater the variability of cash flows from day to day, the greater the attention required.

You have come to the end of your viability study and you should now be able to determine whether your business will be able to sustain itself.

To be viable, an enterprise must be able to generate sustainable profits over the long term and must be able to generate enough money to meet its daily expenses. If it cannot do this, then do not start the enterprise. Look for a new idea and start again.

The next step will be to draw up a **business plan**.

Donald sells hamburgers. He prepared a sales and cash payment estimate as follows:

Month	Sales	Cash payments
January	R5 000	R4 000
February	R6 000	R3 000
March	R4 000	R6 000
April	R2 000	R5 000
May	R2 000	R2 000

Donald notes that:

❏ Fifty per cent of sales are for cash.

❏ The remaining 50 % is collected:
  - half in the first month following sales;
  - the other half the second month after sales.

❏ The beginning cash balance for April is R1 000.

☞

☞❶

Prepare a cash budget for April, May and June.

....

....

....

....

....

....

....

....

10 SUMMARY

To turn a business idea into an enterprise, you must first do a **viability study** to ensure that your business idea will be profitable and that it can maintain a positive cash flow. To do this, you must establish whether your business idea will meet a **need** in the market. You must also assess whether it will be profitable for you to meet that need. To be **profitable** is not enough. You must also be able to manage a positive cash flow. If you cannot meet your expenses on time, you cannot stay in business.

After you have done **market research**, you must define a **mission** for your enterprise. From the mission you must set objectives for your enterprise and then work to attain those objectives. Your mission will indicate **what kind of product and consumer** you should focus on and will enable you to calculate your expected market share. In order to calculate your **expected market share**, you must first determine your **total market potential**, and then your **target market**, and finally your **expected market share**.

After you have done all this, you can calculate your **income** and your **cash flow and profitability**. However, you must first work out your selling price. To fix a **selling price**, you must work out the **cost** of manufacturing the product or providing the service. **All costs** must be **included**. Calculate the cost of placing one unit of your product on the market. You can add a mark-up to the cost price to reach the selling price, but not without taking the selling price of similar products into account.

After calculating the price of your product or service, and knowing what your expected market will be, you can calculate your **total income and net profit**. You must know how far your unit sales can drop before you start showing a loss. This information will help you manage your enterprise better. We call the point at which your enterprise makes **no profit** and **no loss** the **break-even point**.

Finally, you must also draw up a **cash budget**. With the help of the cash budget, you must determine whether you will have enough actual cash available to meet your **running expenses**. The statement will also help you to arrange for finance if and when you need it. Financiers consider the cash budget as very important, because it shows them whether you would be able to meet your financial obligations as they become due.

All these calculations should enable you to determine whether your business idea can be turned into an enterprise. This can be summarised as follows:

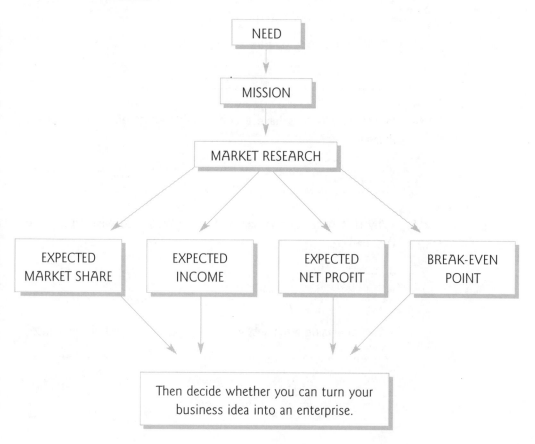

NEED

MISSION

MARKET RESEARCH

EXPECTED MARKET SHARE

EXPECTED INCOME

EXPECTED NET PROFIT

BREAK-EVEN POINT

Then decide whether you can turn your business idea into an enterprise.

11 SELF-EVALUATION

1. Explain why it is important to determine the need for a product.

   ....

   ....

2. How would you find out whether there really is a need for a business idea? Explain step by step.

   ....

   ....

   ....

   ....

   ....

3. Which three key questions will guide you in drawing up a mission statement for your enterprise?

   ....

   ....

   ....

4. Which two factors have a considerable effect on an enterprise's market share?

   ....

   ....

5. Why is it necessary to segment a market if you wish to analyse the market?

   ....

   ....

6. When analysing a market, which segments will you divide it into?

   ....

   ....

   ....

7. Explain each of the following concepts:
    ❑ Fixed costs ....
    ❑ Variable costs ....
    ❑ Total costs ....
    ❑ Direct costs ....
    ❑ Indirect costs ....
    ❑ Overheads ....

8. Calculate the total cost per unit of a product for a manufacturing enterprise. Use the following data:
    ❑ Direct material purchases – R2 000;
    ❑ Direct labour – R3 000;
    ❑ Manufacturing overheads – R1 000;
    ❑ Marketing costs – R1 000;
    ❑ Administrative overheads – R2 000;
    ❑ 10 products were manufactured.

    ....

    ....

9. Use the following information and calculate the selling price of a product.
    ❑ Frank is in a service industry. He works 240 hours per month for 11 months a year. He has expenses per month (for 12 months of the year) totaling R10 000. What must he charge for his services if he wants to make at least a 40% profit?

    ....

    ....

    ❑ Donald sells hamburgers. At what price must he sell his hamburgers if he wants to make a 50% profit, if his costs per hamburger are as follows:
        – direct costs of the materials – R2;
        – direct labour costs – R3;
        – indirect costs – R1.

    ....

    ....

10. Calculate (a) the expected net profit and (b) the break-even point for an enterprise, based on the following information:
    - ❑ Direct material – R8 000 (fruit, sugar, bottles, etc.)
    - ❑ Rent on the factory – R3 000;
    - ❑ Water and power for the factory – R1 000;
    - ❑ Marketing costs – R2 000;
    - ❑ Stationery – R200;
    - ❑ Depreciation on assets – R1 600;
    - ❑ Delivery costs – R3 000;
    - ❑ Salary to owner – R5 000;
    - ❑ Administrative salaries – R2 000;
    - ❑ Direct wages – R12 000;
    - ❑ Telephone – R600;
    - ❑ Water and electricity for the office – R200;
    - ❑ The company can sell 3 000 bottles of preserved fruit a month for at least R15 a bottle.

    ....
    ....
    ....
    ....

11. You have actual sales of R65 000 in June and R60 000 in July. You expect sales of R70 000 in August and R100 000 in September and R100 000 in October. Half of the sales are for cash and the remainder are collected evenly over the following two months. What are your expected cash receipts for August, September and October?

    ....
    ....
    ....
    ....
    ....

12. Your enterprise has sales of R5 000 in March and R6 000 in April. Estimated sales for May, June and July are R7 000, R8 000 and R10 000, respectively. The enterprise has a cash balance of R500 at the beginning of May. Given the following data, prepare and interpret the cash budget for May, June and July.

☞

- ❏ Twenty per cent of your enterprise's sales are for cash; 60% are collected in the next month and the remaining 20% are collected in the second month following sales.
- ❏ The enterprise receives other income of R200 per month.
- ❏ The actual and expected purchases (all for cash) are as follows: R5 000 for May, R7 000 for June and R8 000 for July.
- ❏ Rent is R300 per month.
- ❏ Wages and salaries are 10% of the previous month's sales.
- ❏ A commission of R300 will be paid in June.
- ❏ Payment of principal and interest of R400 on a loan is due in June.
- ❏ A cash purchase of equipment of R600 is scheduled for July.
- ❏ Taxes of R600 are due in June.

....
....
....
....
....
....
....

12 REFERENCES

Brown, C.E., Swanepoel, M.J., De Jong, T.V., Gelderblom, W.C.A., Jordaan, J.F.R. 1994. *Koste- en Bestuursrekeningkunde*. Cape Town: Juta.

Evans, W. 1993. *How to Get New Business in 90 Days and Keep it Forever*. Newtown: Millennium Books.

Hampton, J. & Wagner, C.L. 1989. *Working Capital Management*. New York: John Wiley & Sons.

Harvard Business Review. 1999. *Harvard Business Review on Entrepreneurship*. Boston: Harvard Business School of Publishing.

Kritzinger, A.A.C. & Fourie, J.C.W. 1996. *Basic Principles of Financial Management for a Small Business*. Cape Town: Juta.

Lee, T. 1987. *Cash Flow Accounting*. Berkshire: Van Nostrand Reinhold (UK).

Machado, R. & Cassim, S. 2001. *Marketing Management for Small Business*. 2nd edition. Cape Town: Juta.

Macleod, G. 1999. *Starting your own Business in South Africa*. 9th edition. Cape Town: Oxford University Press.

THE BUSINESS PLAN

1 LEARNING OBJECTIVES (OUTCOMES)

After you have studied this chapter, you must be able to draw up a **business plan**. The business plan must adhere to the following criteria:

❑ It must prove that:
- a sustainable demand for a product/service exists;
- that a sustainable profit can be made from marketing the product/service;
- that the risk involved is reasonable;
- that the entrepreneurial and management teams are experienced and balanced in their composition.
❑ It must be easy to read, concise, factual and practical.

2 INTRODUCTION

In Chapter 4 we learned about the first half of our business planning, namely, how to do a viability study. In this chapter we look at the second half of the planning process: the business plan. If the viability study indicates that your business idea is viable, you will use the business plan to summarise the conclusions drawn from the viability study.

The objective of a business plan is to **communicate** your viable business idea. We communicate with **employees, suppliers, investors, financiers** and other **stakeholders**. (A stakeholder is somebody who has a direct or indirect interest in our business.) The main reason for this communication is to **convince** stakeholders that your new venture will be **successful** and that it is worthwhile to invest in your enterprise. It is important that the business plan communicates the **factors** that are **critical to the success** of every **new venture**, such as:

❑ **The entrepreneurial team**. Who are the members of the team? What do they know? Whom do they know? How well are they known?

❑ **The opportunity**. What will the enterprise sell, and to whom? Can the business grow? How fast? What are the economics, and who and what stand in the way of success?

❑ **The external environment**. Is the entrepreneurial team aware of how changes outside the enterprise can affect its success?

❑ **Risk and reward**. This involves an assessment of everything that can go wrong and right and a discussion of how the enterprise can respond.

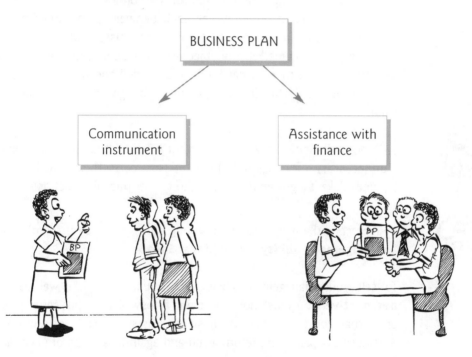

WHO DRAWS UP THE BUSINESS PLAN?

There are **no fixed rules** for **drawing up** a business plan; nor are there fixed rules for **who should draw** it up. However, you will need sound knowledge of the following aspects: the product or service and its potential market; financial management; mercantile and tax legislation. If you lack knowledge in any of these fields, bring in people who have the skills you lack. If you decide to use an outside consultant to write the business plan, it is desirable that the entrepreneurial team stays primarily responsible for the plan. (An entrepreneurial team can consist of yourself alone, you and your spouse or you and your partners, or you and anybody that you wish to engage as part of your team.) The entrepreneurial team's participation usually reflects enthusiasm for the business idea and has the further advantage of being a unifying factor for the team.

4 CONTENTS OF THE BUSINESS PLAN

As already stated, there are no fixed rules according to which a business plan must be drawn up. However, each business plan should at least explain who the entrepreneurial team is; the history of the enterprise and its place in the market; the objectives of the enterprise and what will be done to reach them; what funding is needed and how financing will be redeemed. All this information must be given in a management summary.

Do not write long essays. People do not have the time to work through unnecessary information. Present the facts correctly and stick to the point. Make it a golden rule to stick to two or three lines per point.

Remember, the main reason for writing a business plan is to **sell** your **management ability** and **business idea**.

To sell your management ability, you must present a well-balanced **perspective**. You must not only paint a rosy picture, but must provide proof that you know that any business exists in a state of uncertainty. Your business plan must return again and again to aspects of uncertainty. Important points to address are, among others, the **external environment** and **risk**.

External environment

The entrepreneurial team has **no control over external factors**, yet these can **drastically change the environment** in which you hope to do business. External factors can be government rules and regulations, the level of economic activity, inflation, exchange rates and interest rates. Change in any external environment factor can have a positive or negative effect on the business environment. Point this out in your business plan where applicable, and outline how you are going to address this change.

Risk

Occasionally, a business plan will contain a section devoted to risk. It is better not to focus attention on the risks before you have presented your business plan thoroughly. It is important first to give interested persons a favourable impression of the benefits of your proposed enterprise. However, the aim of the business plan is to encourage people to invest in your business idea. Therefore, they must also know what risks are involved. While working through the business plan, they will ask themselves certain questions:

❑ Who are the people that want me to believe in their business idea?
❑ What are the chances that the enterprise will be successful?
❑ What are the chances that the business will not achieve the expected sales? What will the loss be in such an event, and what is the contingency plan if this happens?
❑ What will happen if the chief supplier of raw materials can no longer supply the raw material? What plan is in place to address this risk?
❑ Will the profits be sufficient and sustainable to warrant the risk of investing in this enterprise?
❑ Would it be better to invest my money in a fixed deposit in a bank?

Deal with these types of questions in the section of the business plan in which they occur. For example, you will have to make a sensitivity analysis of the expected sales in order to address the question of what happens if the business does not achieve its expected sales. (For comparison, refer back to section 8 in Chapter 4.)

Where do I address risk in the business plan?

Throughout the business plan where applicable. Remember always to present a balanced view.

How should I arrange the contents of the business plan?

There is no prescribed way, but you can use the following headings:
* Executive summary
* Entrepreneurial summary
* Description of the enterprise
* Funding requirement
* Addenda

Make a list of possible risks that could arise in the operation of an enterprise. Indicate in which section of the business plan you will address the risk. Also indicate how you will address the risk; in other words, indicate corrective measures.

Risks	Section in the business plan to address the risk	How to address the risk
1.		
2.		
3.		
4.		
5.		
6.		

5 THE ENTREPRENEURIAL TEAM

This part of the business plan deserves special care. Investors focus a lot of their attention here because the skill and experience of the management team together represent a major risk factor. Investors know that most of the market research is estimates. An inexperienced team is more likely to exaggerate the size of the expected market and underestimate the cost factors involved. Therefore it is very important to describe the skills of the management team. The description should pay attention to each member's knowledge of the product or service, the production process, the competitors, the consumers and the external factors that will influence the business environment. Provide a CV for each team member and discuss their relevant experience.

6 DESCRIPTION OF THE ENTERPRISE

Use the following headings to explain where your enterprise is at the moment:
- ❑ **name** of the enterprise;
- ❑ **type** of enterprise;

❏ **type of ownership**;
❏ **primary activity** and **history** of the enterprise;
❏ the **position** of the enterprise within the market;
❏ the **manufacturing plan**;
❏ **location of premises**;
❏ **description** of premises;
❏ **staffing**.

6.1 Name of the enterprise

Give the name of the enterprise. (For information on selecting a name, refer to section 4.3 of Chapter 6.)

6.2 Type of enterprise

Provide information on the type of enterprise. (Please refer to section 3 of Chapter 6.)

6.3 Type of ownership

Provide information on the type of enterprise. (Please refer to section 3 of Chapter 6.)

6.4 Primary activities and history

In this paragraph you must not get bogged down in details. Give the **facts concisely**.
❏ Explain:
   – your business idea in broad terms;
   – what led you to your business idea and how you have developed and tested the idea.
❏ Discuss the problems you have experienced and why those problems will not occur again. You will need to explain:
   – which methods you have used to determine whether the business idea will be viable;
   – the **mission** of your enterprise (Remember, you have already determined this when you did your viability study.);

- how your product or service will **satisfy the needs** of consumers;
- the strengths of your product and how it is positioned in a competitive market;
- the most important **features** of your chief **consumers** and suppliers.

Consider your own business idea. Write a paragraph in a business plan to explain the primary activities of your business idea. (Remember that your description must be brief and businesslike.) Try to limit yourself to about three lines per aspect.

....

....

....

....

....

....

....

....

....

....

....

6.5 The position of the enterprise in the market

Investors and financiers look closely at this section. The **influence** that **competitors** have on the **retention and expansion** of your market share is a **great risk** factor for the success of your enterprise. If competition intensifies, you could lose market share, which will reduce your income. You must **address the fears** of investors and financiers in this paragraph. Be **realistic** with your figures and explain how you did the calculations. Calculating market share is explained in section 5.3 in Chapter 4.

You must describe the **size** and the **target market**, and explain what **sets** your enterprise **apart** from those of your competitors. Because of the importance of this information, it is a good idea to present it under two headings, namely **market analysis** and **competition**.

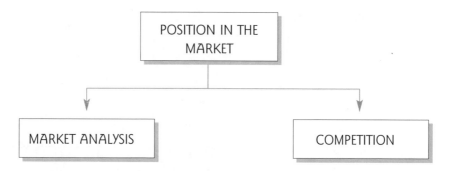

Market analysis

A **proper** market analysis **gives credibility** to your business plan. You must therefore make absolutely sure that your figures are credible. You have already done all the calculations during your viability study when you calculated your potential, target and expected markets (refer to sections 5.1, 5.2 and 5.3 in Chapter 4).

Use your own enterprise/business idea again and do a brief and concise market analysis. Address the following points and try to limit yourself to three lines per point.

- ❑ The total potential demand for your product.
- ❑ Consumer profile.
- ❑ Potential consumers and where they are situated.
- ❑ Your target market.
- ❑ Your expected market share.
- ❑ Your selling price and how it relates to market prices.
- ❑ Your promotion strategy.
- ❑ Your budgeted sales (provide a realistic sales budget as a supplement to the business idea).

....

....

....

....

....

....

....

....

....

.... ☞

☞

....
....
....
....
....
....
....
....
....
....
....
....
....
....

Competition

Explain how your competitors will **influence** your **enterprise**. The purpose of this paragraph is to give a profile of your competitors and how you intend to **manage** the competition. Give a **factually correct** and **balanced image** of your competitors. You should have obtained all the competitor information you need during your viability study. (Refer to section 5 of Chapter 4.) You must now present your findings concisely. Ensure that you **highlight** your competitive advantage. Remember to be realistic as financiers, investors and creditors become suspicious if you portray your competitors as insignificant, or if you exaggerate your market share. Competition is a great risk to your enterprise; if you deal with it realistically, financiers will have confidence in you as a manager. **Highlight problems** and **address** them. Prove that you are a realistic thinker and that you can recognise problems and take corrective steps.

1. Explain briefly:
   (a) what threats your competitors constitute for your enterprise;

   ....
   ....
   .... ☞

(b) what corrective steps you envisage.

....

....

....

6.6 Location of premises

Explain why you have chosen the specific location for the enterprise. (Please refer to section 6 of Chapter 6 for a detailed discussion of this topic.)

6.7 Manufacturing plan

Do this paragraph only if you are going to manufacture a product.

Give:

❏ A short description of the **manufacturing facilities**, the current state of affairs and what expansion will be necessary over the next three years.

❏ A description of the **capital investment** in the manufacturing process and how much will be needed in the next three years.

❏ The **source of raw materials**, what the prices will be, how these will be purchased and stored and how they will be used effectively.

❏ A **list of your suppliers**, stating whether you will be dependent on one supplier. If you are dependent on one supplier, the risk to your enterprise will be greater than if you obtain your raw materials from various suppliers. Banks, creditors and investors will want to know about this risk. Also explain how you plan to reduce the risk.

Do not get bogged down in detailed figures. Explain only the process. All budgets are attached as supplements to the business plan.

The following headings can be used (number your paragraph and write your information briefly and concisely). Remember the guideline – three short lines per point.

The production process

- ❑ Buildings and fixed assets (machinery etc.):
  - – Buildings and fixed-asset requirements;
  - – Life expectancy of buildings and fixed assets;
  - – Depreciation of buildings and fixed assets;
  - – Maintenance of buildings and fixed assets.
- ❑ Design/layout floor plan of the factory;
- ❑ How much of the production capacity will be used;
- ❑ Future production capacity;
- ❑ Raw materials;
  - – Description of raw materials;
  - – Suppliers;
  - – Costs;
  - – Financing and payment;
  - – Availability throughout the year.
- ❑ Labour cost;
  - – How much direct and indirect labour is required;
  - – Availability of labour throughout the year.
- ❑ Production costs per unit.

1. Why is it beneficial to submit a manufacturing plan (as part of the business plan) to financiers, investors and creditors?

   ....

   ....

2. Consider your own business idea/enterprise. Draw up your own manufacturing plan. (Use a separate sheet of paper.)

6.8 Staffing

Your business plan must indicate what the present need for staff is and what it will be in the next three years. Give an indication of the availability of the staff and whether they will be employed part-time or full-time. Indicate the skills the staff possess or must possess and whether they have to be trained. Also give an indication of the staff costs. Include all costs; for example, recruiting staff, training and remuneration.

For each staff member, give a very short CV (about three to four short lines will do). Emphasise the aspects of the staff that will benefit the enterprise, such as their qualifications and experience.

1. What should be discussed in the staff section of the business plan?

   ....

   ....

2. For your own enterprise:
   (a) draw up a staffing budget;
   (b) write the paragraph on staffing in your business plan.

7 THE OBJECTIVES AND STRATEGY OF THE ENTERPRISE

During the viability stage, you studied your product or service, and examined its market, strengths, weaknesses, threats and opportunities. You used this information to decide on a mission and objectives for your enterprise. (If you need to, you can refer to section 4 of Chapter 4.) Revise the work you have done, and give a precise and to-the-point summary under the appropriate headings.

Remember that objectives must be quantifiable, understandable, realistic, time-specific, flexible and consistent. (Refer to section 4 of Chapter 4.) Look at the following two examples.

❑ Sell at least 10 000 products within the first three months of opening the business for trade; increase the sales to 20 000 products over the next three months and to 30 000 and 40 000, respectively, over two further three-month cycles. In total, 100 000 products must be sold within the first year of trading.

❑ Break even within the first year of trading.

Your business strategies must be in place to achieve these objectives.

7.1 Strategy for achieving objectives

This part of the business plan describes the **method** by which your enterprise will operate. A **poorly presented** strategy will make interested parties **doubt the credibility** of your entire business plan. They will not want to invest in your enterprise or enter into partnership.

Refer to the two objectives in the previous paragraph. To achieve these objectives you will need at least the following strategies: marketing, pricing, production, purchasing, staffing, capital acquisition and funding.

(For further information on marketing, pricing, production, purchasing and staff [human resources], please refer to the relevant titles in The Entrepreneurship Series.)

Each of these strategies needs a budget to determine the cost of the strategy. It is usually best to start with the sales budget. The sales budget will determine your income as well as the expenses that must be incurred to achieve the income. The sales budget is usually the only one that reflects income. All the other budgets are expense budgets.

The most commonly used budgets are:
❏ sales budget;
❏ marketing budget;
❏ production budget;
❏ purchasing budget;
❏ personnel budget;
❏ fixed capital budget;
❏ fixed capital acquisition budget.

After completing all the budgets, you need to consolidate them in a pro forma income statement (for more information, refer to section 7 in Chapter 4) and a balance sheet. Of course, all the figures you work with will be projected (estimated) amounts. The risk factor for not achieving your targets is therefore quite high. Do sensitivity analysis where applicable, especially where income must be determined (refer to Chapter 4) and include the results in your business plan.

Also submit your break-even analysis. Not breaking even is a great risk to any business. Provide a contingency plan in the event that you do not break even. This will give proof to your reader that you are a responsible manager who can think and plan ahead.

Prepare cash-flow projections. Also provide contingency plans in the event that you are unable to maintain the minimum cash balance. Remember to include sensitivity analysis for the projected income.

For more information on this topic, refer to A.A.C. Kritzinger & J.C.W. Fourie, *Basic Principles of Financial Management for a Small Business* (Juta).

1. Write down the strengths, weaknesses, opportunities and threats of your new enterprise.

    ....

    ....

    ....

2. Draw up a mission statement for your enterprise.

3. Write down at least three requirements that a properly defined objective should have.

    ....

    ....

    ....

4. Write down three properly defined objectives for your enterprise.

    ....

    ....

    ....

    ....

FUNDING REQUIREMENTS

A word of warning: you need a sound financial background to make the right funding decisions. It would be worth your while to use the services of a competent financial accountant. Even if you do your own calculations, invest in the knowledge of another financial advisor with whom you can discuss your planning and strategies. Wrong decisions taken now may prove costly in future.

Group your costs into operational and fixed costs. This ensures that you fund your expenses from the right sources. You must fund operational costs preferably with short-term funds and capital costs with long-term funds. If you mismatch the type of cost and the source of funding, it could result in serious cash-flow problems at a later stage.

It is also important to determine whether to lease or buy any capital items. Do a capital acquisition budget for this purpose. If you are not very skilled in financial management and income tax legislation, please use skilled people to help you with these calculations.

Let us review the information you have available to help you with your funding decisions:

(a) a full set of budgets;

(b) the total amounts of the costs of your venture;

(c) a pro forma income statement;

(d) a pro forma balance sheet;

(e) all costs grouped into operational and fixed categories;

(f) decision whether to buy or lease fixed assets;

(g) projected profit from your venture;

(h) projected return on investment;

(i) cash-flow projections;

(j) break-even figures.

You must now decide how you want to fund your new venture.

The sources of funds can be:

❑ Internal
  – from the owners of the enterprise;
  – income derived from the operations of the enterprise.

❑ External
  – from loans,
  – leases, etc.

Funds from owners

Owner funds are funds invested in the enterprise and will stay in the enterprise as long as the enterprise exists.

Leading financial institutions require that owners make a significant contribution to the financing of a venture. They regard it as a sound business principle if owners are prepared to take the risk of investing some of their own funds in the enterprise.

The amount of owner funds available will largely depend on the type of ownership of the enterprise. If it is a sole proprietorship, you will be responsible for the total amount of owner funds. If the venture needs more

154

funding than you can provide on your own, you might consider one of the other forms of ownership, such as a partnership, a close corporation or a company. (Please refer to Chapter 6 for more information on this topic.)

Together with your financial advisor, decide on how much owner funds you need and how to obtain it. For information on this subject, refer to A.A.C. Kritzinger & J.C.W. Fourie, *Basic Principles of Financial Management for a Small Business* (Juta).

Before people will invest money (capital) in your venture, they will want to know the answers to certain questions:
- ❑ What will be the return on their investment?
- ❑ How sustainable is the venture?
- ❑ How have you provided for risk?

To answer these questions, explain:
- ❑ the calculation of the estimated profit after taxation;
- ❑ the return on their investment;
- ❑ the sustainability of your market;
- ❑ how you have provided for risk in your planning;
- ❑ the calculation of your sensitivity and break-even analysis;
- ❑ the cash-flow projections;
- ❑ the use of external funds.

You should only use final figures in the explanation, and refer readers to the addenda for detailed calculations.

External financing

External financing is funds you obtain from people who are not owners of the enterprise. You must pay back their money over a specified period.

If you want to obtain financing from outside people, they will want to know whether you will be able to pay them back as specified in the contract.

To answer this question, pay particular attention to:
- ❑ your cash-flow projections;
- ❑ your loan payment schedules (redemption schedule);

❑ who the owners and managers of the enterprise are;
❑ the amount and composition of owner funding;
❑ the security available to serve as collateral for the borrowed funds;
❑ the sustainability of the enterprise;
❑ the management of risk (sensitivity analysis).

Once again, only use final figures in the text, and refer readers to the addenda for detailed information.

Remember the golden rule: be brief and to the point, and provide relevant information only.

1. You need owner funds for your new enterprise. Explain to investors:
   (a) the amount you need and why you need that specific amount;
   (b) the type of owner funding you need;
   (c) how you plan to obtain it.

2. You need external financing for your new enterprise. Explain to financiers:
   (a) why you need it;
   (b) how you plan to obtain it;
   (c) how you plan to redeem it.

9 MANAGEMENT SUMMARY OF THE BUSINESS PLAN

Everyone knows that first impressions are very important. Although the summary is the last part that you write, you place it at the very beginning of your business plan. The summary must be a short and concise presentation of the business plan and must encourage interested parties to devote thorough attention to your plan.

Remember that financiers and investors receive numerous business plans to read. They usually decide while still on the first paragraph whether they are dealing with a successful business plan/business idea.

The summary must indicate on one page:
- ❑ what the enterprise will do (mission);
- ❑ the members of the entrepreneurial team;
- ❑ how the enterprise is placed in its market;
- ❑ where the market is going;
- ❑ the objectives of the enterprise and how these objectives will be attained;
- ❑ how much financing is needed and for what purposes;
- ❑ how the enterprise intends to redeem the financing.

Where the points are discussed, refer the reader to the paragraph in the business plan where the matter is explained in full.

Do not start the summary before you have completed your entire plan. Give this paragraph considerable attention and make use of sketches, graphs and attached brochures where necessary. Inform the interested person fully concerning the product or service that you wish to sell. Your summary should radiate energy and enthusiasm.

Change the management summary to suit the needs of your reader. If it is financing you want, stress the points that financiers are most concerned with, such as the credibility of the entrepreneurial team, sustainability of your market, cash-flow statements and collateral. If you are looking for investment capital, stress the sustainability of income, break-even, risk and return on their investment.

Remember to change your management summary to suit your reader's needs.

Remember that the management summary's most important function is to get and hold your reader's attention.

Write a management summary for your own business idea/enterprise.

10 SUMMARY

The business plan must meet certain requirements:

- ❏ It must prove that:
  - – a sustainable profit can be made from the marketing of the product or service;
  - – that the risk involved is reasonable;
  - – that the management team is experienced and balanced in its composition.
- ❏ The business plan must be concise, factual and clearly presented.
- ❏ It must contain enough information without being wordy. Keep it simple and get to the point. A document that is poorly focused can reveal a lack of management skills. Detailed information can be attached as addenda.
- ❏ It must be a practical document with:
  - – action plans;
  - – budgets;
  - – schedules.
- ❏ It must be easy to read and user-friendly.
  - – Bind the document so there is no loose material.
  - – Provide graphs and pictures to increase the impact of the document, but avoid unnecessary decorations. Always try to produce a neat, businesslike document.
- ❏ The paragraphs must be numbered.
- ❏ The first paragraph of the business plan must be a management summary. Its purpose is to focus the attention of the reader on the business idea and its profitability.
- ❏ The content of the business plan must:
  - – describe the position of the enterprise within the market, the **size of the market** and how this was determined;
  - – indicate the **expected sales** and how this was calculated. Also give the cost of sales per unit;
  - – discuss the competitors and the enterprise's relationship with its competitors;
  - – discuss the weaknesses (risks) of the enterprise openly and indicate how these will be managed.
  - – address risk under the points where it occurs. Do not use a separate heading for weaknesses;
  - – clearly indicate the mission of your enterprise, and that you know exactly which needs your products or services will satisfy.
- ❏ Explain the amount and type of funding you need.
- ❏ Explain the contribution of owner funding and the collateral available as security for external funds.

Although the management summary is the first paragraph of the business plan, it is written after you have completed the rest of the business plan.

EXAMPLE OF A BUSINESS PLAN
A business plan can include the following parts:

I. FRONT PAGE
Provides the:
- ❏ name of the enterprise;
- ❏ logo or emblem of the enterprise;
- ❏ type of enterprise;
- ❏ address and telephone number of the enterprise;
- ❏ owner (name, address and telephone numbers);
- ❏ bankers (name, address and telephone numbers);
- ❏ attorneys (name, address and telephone numbers);
- ❏ auditors (name, address and telephone numbers);
- ❏ date on which the business plan is submitted.

2. A TABLE OF CONTENTS WITH PAGE REFERENCES

3. THE MANAGEMENT SUMMARY

4. THE ENTREPRENEURIAL TEAM

5. THE DESCRIPTION OF THE ENTERPRISE
- ❏ **Primary activities and history of the enterprise:**
    - – mission;
    - – choice and development of the product and problems experienced;
    - – method used to determine the viability of the business idea;
    - – needs of the consumers that the product satisfies;
    - – strengths and weaknesses of the product;
    - – position compared with competing products, opportunities and threats;
    - – features of chief competitors;
    - – features of suppliers;
    - – place of establishment (refer to Chapter 6 for the establishment of an enterprise).

- ❏ **Positioning of the enterprise in the market**
- ❏ Market analysis: ☞

- potential demand;
- consumer profile;
- target market;
- expected market share;
- selling price;
- promotion strategy;
- sales volume.
❑ Competition:
- competitor's profile;
- competitive advantage/edge;
- management of competitors.

❑ **Manufacturing plan**
❑ The production process
❑ Buildings and fixed assets (machinery, etc):
- buildings and fixed assets needed;
- financing and payment;
- life expectancy of buildings and fixed assets;
- maintenance of buildings and fixed assets;
- depreciation.
❑ Design of the factory
❑ How much of the production capacity will be used
❑ Raw materials:
- description of raw materials;
- description of suppliers;
- costs;
- financing and payment;
- availability throughout the year.
❑ Labour:
- how much direct and indirect labour is needed;
- labour costs;
- availability of labour throughout the year;
- what the factory's overhead costs will be;
❑ Production costs per unit
❑ Factory overhead costs

❑ **Staffing**
❑ Current personnel need
❑ Levels of skill

- ❏ Training
- ❏ Availability
- ❏ Staffing costs (staff budget can be attached as supplement)
- ❏ Curricula vitae (CVs) of staff

6. OBJECTIVES AND STRATEGY OF THE ENTERPRISE

- ❏ Objectives
- ❏ Strategies for achieving objectives:
    - – marketing strategy;
    - – pricing strategy;
    - – production strategy;
    - – purchasing strategy;
    - – staffing strategy;
    - – capital acquisition;
    - – funding strategy.
- ❏ Total costs of strategies
- ❏ Fixed costs and operational costs

7. FUNDING REQUIREMENTS

- ❏ Owner portion:
    - – amount of capital (equity) required;
    - – return on equity.
- ❏ Loans from owners:
    - – interest and redemption schedule.
- ❏ Management of risk

- ❏ External funding:
    - – loans;
    - – leasing;
    - – creditors;
    - – security available to cover debt (collateral);
    - – redemption schedule;
    - – cash-flow projections;
- ❏ Management of risk:
    - – break-even analysis;
    - – sensitivity analysis.
- ❏ Ratio analysis

8. ADDENDA

Include all detailed calculations as addenda.

❏ A full set of budgets:
  - sales budget;
  - marketing budget;
  - production budget;
  - purchasing budget;
  - personnel budget;
  - fixed capital budget;
  - fixed capital acquisition budget.

❏ The total amount of the costs of your venture:
  - all costs grouped into operational and fixed costs

❏ A pro forma income statement:
  - projected profit from your venture;
  - projected return on investment.

❏ A pro forma balance sheet:
  - total equity;
  - total long-term debt (liabilities);
  - total operational debt (liabilities);
  - total long-term assets;
  - total operational assets;

❏ Cash-flow projections
❏ Break-even figures
❏ Ratio analysis

SELF-EVALUATION

1. Study the business plan of Happiness Travel and Tours.

   (a) List all the weak points of the business plan, and explain why they are weak points.

   ....
   ....
   ....

(b) List all the strong points of the business plan, and explain why they are strong points.

....

....

....

(c) Rewrite the business plan to eliminate all the weak points.

BUSINESS PLAN OF HAPPINESS TRAVEL AND TOURS

DETAILS OF ENTERPRISE

TYPE OF ENTERPRISE providing a traveling and touring service

ADDRESS OF ENTERPRISE
Address: 16 Church Street, Cresthaven, PRETORIA 2000.
Tel: (011) 611-7111
Fax: (011) 611-7111

OWNER: Betty Falati
Address: 16 Church Street, Cresthaven, PRETORIA 2000.
Tel: (011) 611-7111

BANK: ABSA
Address: Cresthaven, PRETORIA 2000.
Tel: (011) 611-8456
Fax: (011) 611-1234

ATTORNEYS: RICHARDSON & RICHARDSON
Address: Field Street, Cresthaven, PRETORIA 2000.
Tel: (011) 611-4546
Fax: (011) 611-8765

AUDITORS: VAN ZYL, FALATI & SONO
Address: Cresthaven Court, Cresthaven, PRETORIA 2000
Tel: (011) 611-9056
Fax: (011) 611-7771

DATE OF SUBMISSION: 31 APRIL 2003

PURPOSE OF ENTERPRISE

The purpose of the enterprise is to provide transport to tourists who require any of the following services:

❑ day tours in and around Gauteng;

❑ package tours to Sun City and Kruger National Park.

EXECUTIVE SUMMARY

The name of the company is Happiness Travel and Tours. The business will be located in Pretoria. It will be a close corporation. Betty Falati will manage it. For more information on the owners, refer to Addendum A.

OBJECTIVES

❑ To make a turnover of R250 000 in the second year of operations.

❑ To expand my target market into the competitor's market within one year.

The business requires total capital of R175 000. All of the capital will be financed by means of borrowed funds using personal insurance policies as collateral. The loan money will be used to:

❑ pay the staff for six months;

❑ pay initial deposit and rental for the first six months;

❑ acquire assets (kombi and office fittings);

❑ pay for initial advertising costs.

BUSINESS INFORMATION

The company's name is Happiness Travel and Tours. It is a close corporation. It is located in Pretoria and offers transport services to tourists. The enterprise will start business on 1 December 20XX.

Business description

The office hours will be from 7:30 to 17:00. Different hours can be agreed by prior arrangement. I expect the business to be at its busiest during vacations and the festive season. There will be a book-keeper who will come in every two months since the business is still small.

Pricing will be set at a mark-up of 50% on cost.

The number of tourists who need the service exceeds the capacity of the enterprise.

BUSINESS HISTORY

I founded the business in March 20XX after noting the increasing numbers of tourists coming to South Africa, especially from countries such as the United Kingdom and the United States.

PERSONNEL AND ORGANISATION

In addition to the manager, there will be four people working for the enterprise:

Driver/operator
Receptionist
Cleaner
Book-keeper

- ❑ Driver with code 10 licence and at least a diploma in travel and tourism.
- ❑ Book-keeper who will come every two months for accounting purposes.
- ❑ Receptionist who will be responsible for all the office work, including answering phones and making reservations for tourists' trips.
- ❑ Cleaner who is responsible for the cleaning of the office, serving tea and making photocopies.

MARKETING INFORMATION

The tourism industry in South Africa is constantly improving. Both the national and international tourist markets are increasing in volume. My strategy for market entry and penetration is to offer competitive prices and a variety of tours that can cater for special interest groups.

MARKET ANALYSIS

Based on total figures for the year ending February 20XX, compared to the same period for the previous year, there has been a 5% growth in the volume of tourists coming into the country.

There is tremendous goodwill towards South Africa throughout the world. With this in mind, my projection is that the numbers of international tourists visiting South Africa can only increase. At the moment there is a strong market drive to position South Africa to host international events such as the 2010 World Cup.

The World Cup marketing drive will heighten the awareness of South Africa as a tourist destination.

In future, I intend to stratify my client base. This is intended to gain market penetration without losing any of the existing client base.

MARKET RESEARCH

The sources for my research were:

Statistics South Africa

The information I received shows that 76% of foreign travelers are holiday-makers. All of them arrive at the Johannesburg International Airport (JIA), but only 45% stay in the Gauteng region. The rest of the tourists are in transit to other destinations in South Africa. Most of the tourists are from North America or Europe.

Out of the total tourists that arrive at JIA, 40% visit Pretoria, Mpumalanga, North West and neighbouring countries like Swaziland. What attracts them most is our wildlife and scenic beauty. They also want to learn about African culture and see South Africa after the advent of democracy.

Satour

From the information I received from Satour, most tourists visit South Africa between October and January. They choose these months because it is winter in North America and Europe. They also come for the South African wildlife, safaris, culture and scenic beauty.

Other tour operators

Most of the operators I contacted could give information over the phone; however none of it was documented or available in hard copy.

COMPETITORS

My competitors are:
- Large companies which hold 60% of the market, such as Impala and Greyhound.
- Medium-size enterprises which hold 20% of the market, such as Drum Beat Safaris, Holiday for Africa and Prisma Travel.
- The small companies which hold 18% of the market.

We intend gaining 20% of the market.

Competitors' strengths
- ❑ Good location
- ❑ Good vehicles and personnel
- ❑ Good reputation
- ❑ Financially sound

Competitors' weaknesses
- ❑ Expensive
- ❑ Long in advance bookings

My enterprise's business strengths
- ❑ Providing high-quality service
- ❑ Aggressive advertising strategy will help gain market share
- ❑ Being flexible and able to respond quickly
- ❑ Giving customers personal attention and keeping promises
- ❑ Twenty-four-hour booking notice

My enterprise's weaknesses
- ❑ Possible ill-treatment of clients by inexperienced staff. To overcome this, we will put in place good staff training programmes and instil high standards of work practice. We will also establish staff ratings by clients and offer our staff incentive schemes for client care.
- ❑ Due to our size we cannot cater for large groups at the moment. We will overcome this as the enterprise expands.

Advantages of location
Pretoria is a good business location to cater for both national and international tourists.

MARKET
Market segmentation
I am planning to compete in two market segments, namely the national and international tourist markets.

Target market
My primary target market is the international tourist segment.

Geographic factor
Since most of my consumers are in the middle to high-income group, I assume they will mostly come from big cities and towns.

Demographic factor

My clients will be of all ages but mostly between the ages of 20 and 65 and from both sexes. They will be from different religions, races, social class and lifestyles. Since they will be outgoing people, I presume they lead a liberal lifestyle and are ambitious.

Service

We will provide a high-quality service. My staff will receive the best possible training in customer care and efficiency. Service will have to be one of our outstanding qualities. Clients will be asked to rate the company for service delivery. The ratings will guide us on areas to improve ourselves.

Promotions

- Promotion through Satour and Pretoria tour operators
- The bus will have the name, logo and slogan of the business
- Advertise on big city billboards and at the JIA
- Place business cards and brochures at some hotels
- Advertise on radio stations

DISTRIBUTION

Because of the type of business, there will not be a distribution channel.

PRICING

It will be a cost plus percentage profit, but will also be market related. I will give seasonal discounts.

MARKETING GOALS

- Secure 10% of the market in my fourth year of operation.
- Reach the R250 000 mark in turnover in the third year of operation.

FINANCIAL INFORMATION
ESTIMATED STARTUP CAPITAL

	MONTHLY EXPENSES	CASH NEEDED TO START	% OF TOTAL	SOURCE OF ESTIMATE
MONTHLY COSTS				
Salaries and wages	R5 000	R15 000	42%	Mag Chri Tours and Safari
Rent	R800	R2 400	7%	Mag Chri Tours and Safari
Advertising	R3 000	R9 000	26%	Mag Chri Tours and Safari
Telephone	R400	R1 200	3%	Mag Chri Tours and Safari
Insurance	R800	R2 400	7%	Auto and General
Maintenance	R200	R600	2%	AA
Miscellaneous	R160	R400	1%	Mag Chri Tours and Safari
Interest	R1 375	R4 125	12%	Standard Bank
Sub-total	R11 735	R35 125		

ONCE-OFF COSTS

Motor vehicle	R110 000	77%	Austen Motors
Furniture	R5 000	4%	Oosthuizen Brothers
Computer equipment	R8 000	6%	Mustek
Equipment	R2 000	1%	Mag Chri Tours and Safari
Decoration and remodelling	R3 000	2%	Mag Chri Tours and Safari
Installation charges	R500	0,4%	Mag Chri Tours and Safari
Deposits with public utilities	R10 000	7%	Mag Chri Tours and Safari

Legal and other professional fees	R700	0,6%	Kunene Inc
Licences and permits	R1 000	1%	Mag Chri Tours and Safari
Advertising and promotion for opening	R2 000	1%	Mag Chri Tours and Safari
Sub-total	R142 200		
TOTAL ESTIMATE FOR STARTUP	**R177 325**		

BUDGET FOR THE FIRST YEAR OF OPERATION

	NOTES		
REVENUES			**R172 500**
Revenues from operations	1	R172 500	
Other revenues			
EXPENSES			**R143 020**
Employee salaries		R60 000	
Rent		R9 600	
Office supplies		R1 920	
Advertising	2	R11 000	
Professional services		R700	
Communications		R4 800	
Insurance		R9 600	
Depreciation		R26 500	
Interest		R16 500	
Other expenses		R2 400	
NET OPERATING INCOME (Before income tax)			**R29 480**
Income tax @ 35%			R10 318
EXCESS INCOME OVER EXPENSES			**R19 162**
Return on investment			11%

Notes:

1. This is based on an average daily income of R500 for 345 productive days.
2. Based on 3 months' advertising costs plus opening promotion and publicity.

BALANCE SHEET

ASSETS		
FIXED ASSETS		**R128 500**
Motor vehicle	R110 000	
Furniture	R5 000	
Equipment	R13 500	
OTHER ASSETS		**R11 000**
License	R1 000	
Deposits	R10 000	
CURRENT ASSETS		**R35 500**
Cash	R35 500	
TOTAL ASSETS		**R174 500**
LIABILITIES AND EQUITY		
EQUITY		**R0**
LONG TERM LIABILITIES		**R150 000**
Long-term loans	R150 000	
CURRENT LIABILITIES		**R25 000**
Short-term loans	R25 000	
TOTAL LIABILITIES AND EQUITY		**R175 000**

ADDENDUM A

CURRICULUM VITAE: BETTY FALATI

PERSONAL DETAILS

Surname	Falati
First names	Betty
Title	Ms

Residential address   16 Church Street
Cresthaven
Pretoria
2000

Postal address	As residential address
Contact number	(011) 611-7111
Date of birth	13 December 1970
Identity number	7012135000007
Nationality	South African
Marital status	Single
State of health	Excellent
Criminal record	None

EDUCATION DETAILS

High school education

Name of school	Tiyelelani Secondary School
Highest standard passed	Matric with exemption
Year achieved	November 1993
Subjects passed	N. Sotho, English, Afrikaans, Mathematics, Physical Science and Biology

Tertiary Education

Name of institution	Technikon Northern Gauteng
Qualification achieved	National Diploma in Tourism
Year achieved	April 1998

Current studies

Name of institution	Technikon Witwatersrand
Qualification enrolled for	B-Tech Degree: Tourism Entrepreneurship IV

Languages

English, Afrikaans, Northern Sotho	Speak, read and write
Zulu, Setswana	Speak and read
Venda, Tsonga and Swazi	Speak

EMPLOYMENT HISTORY

Name of company	Travel and Touring
Duration	April 1998 to date
Position held	Tour operator

2. Draw up a business plan for the enterprise that you are planning. State who will read it and who was involved in drawing it up. Please ensure that your business plan at least conveys:
   ❑ that a sustainable demand for your product exists;
   ❑ that a sustainable profit can be made;
   ❑ that the entrepreneurial and management team is experienced;
   ❑ that the risk involved is reasonable.

Hint: You have already completed certain paragraphs while working through this chapter. Revise the work you have done and use it for the business plan you must now draw up.

12 REFERENCES

Hampton, J.J. *et al.* 1989. *Working Capital Management*. New York: John Wiley & Sons.

Harvard Business Review. 1999. *Harvard Business Review on Entrepreneurship*. Boston: Harvard Business School Publishing.

Kritzinger, A.A.C. & Fourie, J.C.W. 1996. *Basic Principles of Financial Management for a Small Business*. Cape Town: Juta.

Le Roux, E.E. *et al.* 1995. *Business Management: A Practical Approach*. Isando: Heinemann.

Macleod, G. 1999. *Starting Your Own Business in South Africa*. 9th edition. Cape Town: Oxford University Press Southern Africa.

Van Zyl, G. 1996. *Your Own Business: Practical Guidelines for a Business Plan*.

6 SETTING UP A BUSINESS

1 LEARNING OBJECTIVES (OUTCOMES)

After you have studied this chapter, entrepreneurs who are setting up a new business should know:

❑ what are the legal requirements for establishing the proposed business;
❑ what labour legislation should be considered when establishing a business;
❑ what factors should be considered in choosing the form of business;
❑ what procedure must be followed to set up a specific form of business;
❑ what factors should be considered in choosing the place of establishment;
❑ what operating elements of the business functions are essential in the setting-up phase.

2 INTRODUCTION

People who wish to set up a business have learned:

❑ how to analyse themselves critically (i.e. have determined their strengths and weaknesses);
❑ to distinguish the various forms of business;
❑ how to turn a business idea into an opportunity for a new business;
❑ how to do a viability study for the proposed business;
❑ how to draw up a business plan.

These were covered in the evaluation and planning phases.

In the final phase, we examine the practical factors that the entrepreneur must pay attention to in setting up a business.

These include:

❏ the factors that influence the choice of a form of business;
❏ the duties and legal requirements of forms of business;
❏ the procedure for setting up each form of business;
❏ the factors that play a role in the choice of a place of establishment;
❏ the relation between setting-up factors and the various business functions.

3 THE FACTORS THAT INFLUENCE THE CHOICE OF A BUSINESS FORM

There are many important factors to consider when choosing the right business form. Many of these are quite complicated and involve particular legal requirements and procedures. It is best to approach an accountant, auditor or attorney before you decide what form your business will take. The topic is discussed extensively in Cilliers, H.S., Benade, M.L. *et al.* 2000. *Entrepreneurial Law.* 2nd edition. Durban: Butterworth.

Refer back to Chapter 3 for the advantages and disadvantages of different business forms.

In this chapter we will look at the following factors:

❏ The **nature of the product or service** that is offered;
❏ The **legal liability** of the owners;
❏ The **business form** and how it is affected by **income tax**;
❏ The specific **legal requirements**.

These are not the only factors, but they are certainly some of the most important ones.

3.1 The nature of the product or service

The nature of the product, as well as the complexity of its development, manufacture and marketing, will determine which business form is the most suitable. A business that manufactures security gates requires the involvement of one or two owners, a few employees and possibly a garage as workshop, and the minimum of equipment.

175

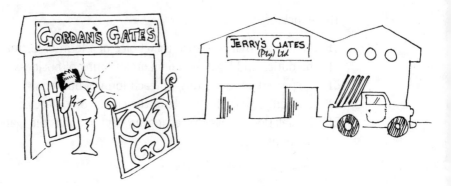

For this type of business a sole proprietorship or partnership will be sufficient. If this business sets up a factory to manufacture remote-controlled gates and doors for residential and industrial use, then it is advisable to consider a more sophisticated business form, like a close corporation or a private company.

3.2 The legal liability of the owners

The close corporation and company possess their own legal personality, while the **sole proprietor** and the **partnership** do not.

This means that the person in the sole proprietorship and the members of a partnership are usually responsible for the tax and debt obligations/commitments of the business. They therefore have **unlimited liability** for commitments of the business.

The shareholders of **companies** and members of **close corporations** have limited liability in respect of commitments of the particular business form. The person can therefore be held **responsible to a limited extent** for the commitments of the company or close corporation.

3.3 The business form and the effect of taxation on it

In many cases, the effect of income tax determines the choice of the most suitable business form. The tax policy changes frequently, for example when concessions or increased tax for certain groups are announced in the annual budget by the Minister of Finance. (In 1999, the tax rate for companies and close corporations was reduced to 30% to encourage business investment and development. The tax rate on dividends is 12,5%.)

3.4 Specific legal requirements

It is important to know what the legal requirements of the various business forms are. In the case of a company, a Deed of Establishment must be registered with the Registrar of Companies, and financial statements must be drawn up and approved annually by a chartered accountant. Certain sole proprietors and partnerships, like restaurants, must renew their licences annually. Others, like nursery schools, do not have to. Where, for example, health inspectors have to make inspections and there are health risks, annual renewal must take place. These are a few examples of the types of legal requirements that need attention.

It is important to collect as much information as possible to determine the most suitable form for the proposed business.

You can get information by reading books or making use of experts, like attorneys, auditors or business consultants.

Describe, in one or two sentences, each of the four important factors that influence the choice of a business form:

1. The nature of the product or service that is offered:

....

2. The degree of legal liability of the owners:

....

3. The business form and the effect of income tax on it:

....

4. The specific legal requirements:

....

4   THE DUTIES AND LEGAL REQUIREMENTS OF BUSINESS FORMS

The duties and legal requirements that apply to all business forms include:

- ❑ that the person is of full legal capacity;
- ❑ that the type of economic activity that will be undertaken is explicitly stated;
- ❑ that the name of the business is accepted;
- ❑ that the registration of patents, trademarks and designs is carried out;
- ❑ that testing of products takes place;
- ❑ that licensing is done;
- ❑ that registration with the Receiver of Revenue takes place;
- ❑ that registration with the Commissioner for Unemployment Insurance takes place;
- ❑ that registration with the appropriate local authority takes place;
- ❑ that registration with the Department of Commerce and Industry takes place;
- ❑ that the business complies with the general industrial and commercial legislation.

We will briefly discuss each duty and legal requirement. The relevant bodies can provide all the information you need.

4.1 Full legal capacity

An insolvent person or a person under judicial management may not set up a business. The risk involved in entrepreneurship often causes entrepreneurs to lose everything. Think of the example of Henry Ford in Chapter 1. Entrepreneurs with limited trading competence is limited often manage to run a business somehow and do it in the name of a spouse or family member.

4.2 The type of economic activity

The requirements differ in respect of various types of businesses that are set up. Applicable laws and requirements (for example, in respect of hygiene and safety) must be complied with in businesses such as bakeries, insurance brokers, restaurants, bottle stores, manufacturing businesses, construction firms, etc. It is important to establish which requirements and legal duties must be fulfilled before you can set up a business.

Find out from the **municipality** or **licensing authority** where you intend establishing the business which legal obligations you have to fulfil to establish a business in the specific area.

4.3 Naming

The law governing business names **limits the choice** of names. The trading name of a business must be approved to protect businesses and avoid duplication. The names of companies are approved by the Registrar of Companies. The registration protects the company so that other businesses do not use the same name.

The choice of a name must comply with the Business Names Act, 1960 (No. 27 of 1960). The letters 'cc' must, for example, appear at the end of the name of a close corporation. (Proprietary) Limited/(Eiendoms) Beperk or (Pty) Ltd/(Edms) Bpk must appear at the end of the name of a private company.

4.4 Registration of patents, trade marks and designs

Entrepreneurs can patent unique products, services, trade marks or designs. Registration of patents is performed by a **patents attorney**. Annual registration fees are payable after three years so that the registered patent does not expire. Trade marks of products are registered at the trade marks office in Pretoria. A design which gives exclusive rights to form and colour combinations, among other aspects, can be registered with the designs office. Registered trade marks are valid for 10 years.

4.5 Testing

Products can be tested by the **South African Bureau of Standards** (SABS). It is sometimes also a requirement of contracts that products are manufactured in accordance with the specifications of the SABS.

4.6 Licensing

The purpose of the Business Act 71 of 1991 is mainly to ensure deregulation, in other words, the minimum regulations. This makes it easier to establish a business. The Act has been under discussion and may change. The process is complicated because local authorities earn an income from licensing fees, and are not in favour of the deregulation that will reduce their source of income.

Approach the **local authority** to find out the regulations and rules regarding licensing in a particular area.

4.7 Registration with the Receiver of Revenue

The new business must be registered with the Receiver of Revenue and tax must be paid:

- ❑ as employer;
- ❑ as taxpayer;
- ❑ on added value (VAT).

1. As **employer**, the business must collect the employees' tax and pay it to the Receiver (for example, the payment of SITE and PAYE tax).

2. As **taxpayer**, the business or the owner (depending on the type of business under discussion) must pay tax on net income annually. Businesses make provision for income tax by the payment of provisional tax.

3. Businesses that have an annual turnover of more than R150 000 must register with the Receiver of Revenue for payment of **value-added tax**. It is important to obtain the information concerning the calculation and payment of VAT before you set up a business. Thorough planning and administration of the business can avoid fines and other problems.

Value-added tax is based on the following principles:

❑ VAT must be included in the **selling price** of your product or service by you as entrepreneur, and paid by your client. The business therefore receives VAT on **sales**.

❑ When a business produces products and/or services, the business pays for raw materials, other material, products and services to make the manufacturing and provision possible. The business therefore pays VAT on **purchases**.

❑ The difference between the **VAT that has been paid** and the **VAT that has been collected** must be paid monthly by the business to the Receiver of Revenue, or claimed back.

Consult an accountant or the local Receiver of Revenue for information on the registration of employees, the provision for the payment of income tax and the payment and claiming of VAT.

4.8 Registration for unemployment insurance

An employer is obliged by the Unemployment Insurance Act 30 of 1966 to make contributions to the Unemployment Insurance Fund. Employees in the lower income groups qualify in terms of this law for payment of unemployment insurance by the employer. When employees resign, are dismissed or take maternity leave, they are assured of a monthly income for a certain number of months.

4.9 Registration with the Workmen's Compensation Commissioner

A business must register as an employer with the Workmen's Compensation commissioner **within 14 days** of commencing business.

The registration is compulsory in terms of the Workmen's Compensation Act 30 of 1941 (as amended). Employees in a particular income group are compensated when, as a result of an accident or injury, they can no longer earn an income. Employers pay the Workmen's Compensation Commissioner an annual amount calculated according to the income of the employees.

4.10 Registration with local authorities

Businesses may have to pay **service levies** and **turnover levies** to the local authorities. The service levy is a percentage of the amount that is paid in salaries and wages, and the turnover levy is a percentage of the turnover of the business.

4.11 Registration with the Department of Commerce and Industry

A **new manufacturing business** must register with the Department of Trade and Industry (DTI). Businesses that require import permits are also obliged to register with the DTI.

4.12 General industrial and commercial legislation

Businesses must comply with the industrial legislation that is applicable to them. Examples are the Occupational Health and Safety Act and the Wage Act (which prescribes minimum wages in cases where industrial agreements do not exist).

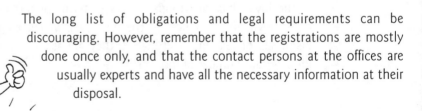

The long list of obligations and legal requirements can be discouraging. However, remember that the registrations are mostly done once only, and that the contact persons at the offices are usually experts and have all the necessary information at their disposal.

1. Who is not allowed to set up a business?

....

2. Why do you have to register the name of your business?

....

3. Why are employers obliged to make contributions to the Unemployment Insurance Fund?

....

4. To whom (which body) must businesses pay service levies and turnover levies?

....

5 LABOUR LEGISLATION

Most small businesses depend on employees, so knowledge of, and adherence to, labour legislation is important when you start your own business. Labour legislation balances the power between employers and employees and is intended to protect both parties in the employment relationship. The legislation pertaining to this relationship is extensive, and there is not enough space here to discuss all of it in detail. However, you can easily obtain the relevant Acts (see section 5.2 for telephone numbers and addresses). In this section, we will look at each Act briefly to ensure that you have a basic awareness of requirements that might be of concern to your planned business.

5.1 Employment contracts

In an employment contract the employee makes his/her services available to an employer. The employer describes the duties to be performed by the employee and they agree on a wage or salary. The employer/employee relationship comprises certain rights and obligations that have to be mutually agreed upon. The contract defines whether employment is for a fixed or indefinite period. There are three forms of contract:

❑ written contracts;
❑ verbal contracts;
❑ tacit contracts.

Written contracts

The duties and obligations of the employer and employee are included in a written contract, for example:

- remuneration;
- leave (annual, sick, maternity or other);
- working hours;
- protection of the interests of the company (for example, restraint of trade clauses);
- job title and position;
- medical aid;
- pension fund membership.

The Basic Conditions of Employment Act 75 of 1997 determines specific requirement with regard to employment contracts. The Act requires that at least 20 particulars, as stipulated in Section 29, must be reflected in your contract.

For detailed information, a copy or a summary of the Basic Conditions of Employment Act can be obtained from the address in section 5.2 or from http://www.polity.org/govdocs/regulations/1998/reg98-1438.html.

An example of a contract of employment is included at the end of this chapter as Addendum 1.

Verbal contracts

This type of contract is a verbal agreement between the employer and employee. Although verbal contracts are binding, this form of contract is not recommended, because in a dispute judgement has to be made on the word of one person against another.

Tacit contract

The terms of the contract and conditions of employment are determined by the past behaviours of the employer and employee, respectively. This situation is not advisable, because past behaviour might not be interpreted in the same way by the employer and the employee.

Let us look at an example: an employee is employed at a specific salary as a full-time employee, but due to a low workload eventually works half-days only. After a year the situation at the business changes and the employer expects the employee to work a full day at the salary agreed upon when the appointment was made. The tacit agreement of working half-days only can be seen as binding by the employee and he/she can dispute the employer's changed expectations of reverting to full-day work.

5.2 Labour Relations Act 66 of 1995

The Labour Relations Act (LRA) aims to establish co-determination in the workplace. The aim is to transform the relationship between management and labour from being adversarial to being co-operative, from fragmented dealings with one another to ongoing interaction, and from distributive to a more integrative approach.

The complete Act can be obtained from the following address:

Government Printer
Bosman Street
Private Bag X85
Pretoria 0001

Tel: (012) 334-4500
Fax: (012) 323-0009

http://www.polity.org/govdocs/legislation/1995/act95-066.html.

The primary objectives of the Act are to:
❑ regulate the fundamental rights of all South Africans;
❑ promote collective bargaining and collective agreements;
❑ promote participation of workers in the workplace;
❑ promote the resolutions of disputes.

Regulation of fundamental rights

This section of the Act refers to:

❑ **Freedom of association**, which guarantees the rights of employees and employers to form or belong to a trade union or employers' organisation. They may then also participate in the lawful activities of these organisations, participate in elections and be elected as office-bearers or officials. For an example of an employers' organisation (which you can join when you establish your business), refer to the last part of section 5.5.

❑ **Organisational rights**, which means the right of the trade union with regard to:
- access to the workplace;
- deductions of trade union levies from members' wages;
- reasonable leave for trade union activities for office-bearers during working hours;
- disclosure of some information.

The employees are protected against:

❑ **unfair dismissal** (sections 185–197), which determines that an employee can be dismissed for a valid reason only, and a fair procedure has to be followed;

❑ **unfair labour practice** (Schedule 7, Part B), which includes promotion, demotion, discrimination and disciplining of employees;

❑ **strikes and lockouts** (sections 64–77), which refers to the right of employees to strike and of employers to lock employees out.

Promotion of collective bargaining (sections 23–63)

The Labour Relations Act aims to promote constructive co-operation between management and labour and includes:

❑ collective agreements;
❑ agency shop agreements;
❑ closed shop agreements;
❑ collective bargaining beyond the workplace;
❑ establishment, powers and functions of bargaining councils;
❑ statutory councils.

Promotion of worker participation (sections 78–94)

This enables workers to participate in the running of a business through negotiations, institutionalised consultation and joint decision-making.

Workplace forums can be formed only in enterprises with more than 100 employees.

Promotion of dispute resolution

The Labour Relations Act promotes resolution of disputes at the business level, but provides procedures and support structures for the resolution of labour disputes through conciliation, mediation and arbitration.

The Commission for Conciliation, Mediation and Arbitration (CCMA) is established in terms of Section 112 of the LRA. It is independent of government, political parties, trade unions, employers, employees' organisation, trade union federations or employers' organisations.

The functions of the CCMA are as follows:

❑ Resolve through conciliation any disputes referred to it in terms of the LRA.
❑ Arbitrate disputes not resolved through conciliation, if determined to do so by the LRA and all parties involved.
❑ Assist in the establishment of workplace forums.
❑ Compile and publish information and statistics about its activities.

5.3 Basic conditions of Employment Act 75 of 1997

The purpose of the Act is to give effect to the right to fair labour practices referred to in section 23(1) of the Constitution. This is done by establishing and making provision for the regulation of basic conditions of employment. The Basic Conditions of Employment Act provides for the right to reasonable and fair minimum conditions of employment.

The most important provisions of the Act are:

❑ a 45-hour working week, (Section 9) and procedures to achieve a 40-hour working week;
❑ maximum overtime (Section 10) of 3 hours a day and 10 hours a week;
❑ rate for overtime (Section 10 [2]) to be paid at one-and-a-half times the normal wage;
❑ rest period (Section 15) of at least 12 consecutive hours daily;
❑ Sunday work (Section 16) to be paid at double the normal rate;
❑ night work (Section 17);
❑ paid leave (Section 20[1][a]) set at 21 consecutive days after 12 months/ 1 day for every 17 days worked/1 hour for every 17 hours worked;
❑ proof of incapacity with a medical certificate (Section 23);
❑ maternity leave (Section 25) set at four months, with a possibility of the Unemployment Insurance Fund financing this leave;
❑ family responsibility leave (Section 27) set at three days per year, after being employed for four months;
❑ notice of termination (Section 37);

❏ written particulars of employment (Section 29). The Act requires that at least 20 particulars, as stipulated in Section 29, must be reflected in your contract. (See Addendum I for an example of a contract of employment.)

For further information, a copy or a summary of the Basic Conditions of Employment Act 75 of 1997 can be obtained from the address in section 5.2 or at http://www.polity.org/govdocs/regulations/1998/reg98-1438.html.

5.4 Employment Equity Act 60 of 1998

The purpose of the Act is to eliminate unfair discrimination by providing equal opportunities, fair treatment in employment and affirmative action in appointments and promotion.

The Act prohibits discrimination against employees and job applicants on the basis of race, gender, pregnancy, marital responsibility, ethnic or social origin, sexual orientation, age, disability, HIV status, religion, conscious belief, political opinion, culture, language and birth.

Affirmative action measures apply to employers:

❏ employing 50 employees or more;
❏ employing less than 50 employees but where the enterprise has an annual turnover that is equal to or above the applicable minimum annual turnover in terms of the following Schedule of the National Small Business Act 102 of 1996.

SECTOR OR SUBSECTORS IN ACCORDANCE WITH THE STANDARD INDUSTRIAL CLASSIFICATION	TOTAL ANNUAL TURNOVER
Agriculture	R2,00m
Mining and Quarrying	R7,50m
Manufacturing	R10,00m
Electricity, Gas and Water	R10,00m
Construction	R5,00m
Retail and Motor Trade and Repair Services	R15,00m
Wholesale Trade, Commercial Agents and Allied Services	R25,00m
Catering, Accommodation and Other Trades	R5,00m
Transport, Storage and Communications	R10,00m
Finance and Business Services	R10,00m
Community, Social and Personal Services	R5,00m

Affirmative action determines that suitably qualified applicants/employees from the following designated groups should be employed/promoted:

❑ Africans;
❑ Coloureds;
❑ Asians;
❑ women;
❑ disabled.

5.5 Skills Development Act 97 of 1998

The aim of the Skills Development Act is to ensure that the education, training and development needs of employees are addressed by employers. Employers have to pay a skills development levy of 1 per cent of their annual wages and salaries to the National Skills Fund. When employees are trained or receive education, according to specifications, a percentage (up to 80 per cent of the 1 per cent paid) of their contribution will be paid back to the business. It is important to note that only those small businesses with total salary and wage bills of more than R250 000 will be required to pay the skills development levy.

For more detailed information on the Acts relevant to small businesses, refer to Amos, T. & Ristow, A. 1999. *Human Resource Management.* Juta: Cape Town.

As an employer, it is also advisable to become a member of an employers' organisation, such as the Confederation of Employers of Southern Africa (COFESA). COFESA protects employers' rights and provides a service to employers by translating legal jargon into user-friendly practice. Services include:

❑ a practical manual covering Acts, contracts, disciplinary procedures and procedures for fair labour relations;
❑ a 24-hour hotline to prevent expensive litigation;
❑ consultants.

Contact COFESA at:

PO Box 300, Florida Hills 1716

Tel: (011) 679-4373   Fax: (011) 679-4393

http://www.cofesa.co.za

6 THE PROCEDURE WHEN SETTING UP EACH FORM OF BUSINESS

In this section, we will look at the different procedures to follow for setting up various forms of business.

6.1 The sole proprietorship and the partnership

Few legal requirements govern the setting-up of a sole proprietorship and a partnership.

The laws and regulations discussed in section 4 apply to these businesses.

A partnership is formed by a written or oral agreement between the partners. If the partners sign a written agreement, the Stamp Duties Act 77 of 1968 provides that the contract must be stamped.

6.2 The company

The Companies Act 61 of 1973 also prescribes the way to set up a company. This Act consists of 443 articles, plus addenda, and prescribes 52 procedures.

The registration and creation of a company is performed by the office of the Registrar of Companies in Pretoria.

The steps in setting up a company are:

1. **Reserve a name for the company** to ensure that the name that is chosen is not already being used by another company. The name must also by law be acceptable to the Registrar of Companies. Form CM 5 of the Companies Act is used for this purpose.

2. **A Memorandum of Association and statutes/articles must be drawn up.** A chartered accountant or attorney can be appointed to do this. Each signatory of the Memorandum of Association receives a certain number of shares and the number of shares is recorded alongside the name of the signatory. There is only one shareholder in a one-person company. The signatories of the Memorandum of Association also sign the statutes.

3. The following **documents and information** must be submitted to the Registrar of Companies for the registration of a company:

❑ Details of the reserved or approved name, the translation of the name, or a shortened form, if applicable (form CM 7 of the Companies Act).

❑ Two copies of the **Memorandum of Association and statutes** that have been signed as prescribed, over and above the original Memorandum of Association and statutes.

❑ Information concerning **the situation of the registered office** and postal address (form CM 22 of the Companies Act).

❑ Written **acceptance by a chartered accountant** who is prepared to audit the annual financial statements.

❑ **Annual duty** of R80 must accompany the application at registration, except in the case of a Section 21 company.

❑ **Proof that the registration fee has been paid** must be provided.

4. The Registrar of Companies endorses a certificate that the company has been incorporated. The **certificate of incorporation** indicates that the company has received a legal personality.

6.3 The close corporation

Registration and control of close corporations is performed by the Registrar of Close Corporations in Pretoria. Provisions and guidelines are prescribed by the Close Corporations Act 69 of 1984 (as amended).

There are various types of applicants for close corporations:

❑ a company that wishes to act as a close corporation in future;

❑ a dormant body that was previously registered as a close corporation and wishes to reregister must apply for "Renewal of Registration";

❑ the purchase of a dormant close corporation by new members;

❑ a first registration.

The services of an accountant or attorney can be used to create a close corporation. The following documents and information are required when a close corporation is created:

1. Completion of the founding statement

A founding statement must be completed on form CK 1. Details of the close corporation and the names of the members must be stated on the form.

2. Submission of the founding statement

The completed founding statement is submitted to the Registrar of Close Corporations in triplicate. Revenue stamps of R80 and the signature of each member must appear on the founding statement.

3. The registration of the close corporation

The Registrar of Close Corporations awards a registration number once all the requirements of the Close Corporations Act have been fulfilled. The registration number is entered on the founding statement. The Registrar also issues a Certificate of Incorporation. The close corporation has then legally come into existence and this is announced in the *Government Gazette* by the Registrar. Henceforth the close corporation is a legal person and can start business operations.

The process of founding a close corporation is simpler than founding a company.

Existing dormant companies and close corporations can be bought. Make inquiries with an auditor, attorney or accountant, as they are usually aware of available companies or close corporations. This is a quicker and easier method of registration, but you will usually have to pay a premium for this convenience.

Four individuals realise that there are opportunities in the South African construction industry (especially for low-cost housing). They investigate the situation to identify business opportunities. Low-cost housing is the immediate need and their first priority is to obtain cheap raw materials. They look into the use of heaps of ash from burnt coal at power stations. Tests have been done by mixing the ash with a binding agent (resin) and compressing it. The result is that it can be used as roofing sheets, similar to asbestos sheets. An additional advantage of the new product is that it is stronger than asbestos, as it does not break if it falls, as asbestos does. The roofing sheets can also be pasted straight on to the brickwork, using a special adhesive.

☞

It is an ideal product for low-cost housing and the innovative businessmen decide to manufacture the new product to satisfy the existing need.

1. Which business form will be the most suitable for the proposed business?

    ....

    ....

2. Give reasons for your choice.

    ....

    ....

    ....

3. What procedure will you follow to set up the business? Discuss briefly.

    ....

    ....

    ....

    ....

7 FACTORS THAT PLAY A ROLE IN THE CHOICE OF THE PLACE OF ESTABLISHMENT

There are many factors that play a role in identifying a place of establishment for the business. There are different considerations for a commercial business and manufacturing business. It is important to choose the right place of establishment, but it is the entrepreneur's responsibility to take a considered decision in respect of a place of establishment. It is a good idea to read widely on the topic, to make inquiries and ask experts or advice.

Consider the following when choosing a place of extablishment:

❑ The **market**. This is especially important in the case of a trading enterprise where the business must be visible to the target market; in other words the business must be near the market and easily accessible;

❑ **Access to raw materials** is particularly important to manufacturing businesses. Remember: in this case you must ☞

determine whether it is more important to be close to the market or close to raw materials. The types of raw materials and the type of final product will determine this choice (for example, in the case of the roof sheeting manufacturers, the factory is built near the power stations so that the heaps of coal ash do not have to be transported too far);

❑ Availability of suitable **human resources or labour**;

❑ The **costs** involved in hiring or renting the building and how it compares with other possibilities. Also compare it to those of competitors. Remember, the cheapest is not always the best;

❑ **Climate**. The climate is important in the establishment of a business. A business that produces leather outfits for men and ladies and is established in Durban will sell fewer outfits in this environment than a person who sets up the same type of business in Cape Town;

❑ Find out about **regional incentive programmes**. To encourage development in particular regions or industries, the government promotes industrial incentive schemes. These entail, for example, the availability of financing for building factories in certain areas, reduced taxation for a specific period, etc. Contact the Department of Trade and Industry and local authorities for more information. The roof sheeting factory will, for example, qualify for an incentive subsidy if it is erected in a designated area;

❑ Take note of factors like the availability of **public transport systems** – roads, harbours, train services, airports – **water supply**; **parking space**; **electricity** and **support services** of other businesses in the area that you are considering;

❑ **Personal and social considerations**. These are often the most important factors in the choice of a place of establishment. The entrepreneur must ensure that all the factors mentioned above are considered and that a choice is not made simply on the strength of personal preference.

It is important to determine the best place to establish a specific type of business, because this will influence the competitiveness of the business. Market research and a thorough study are therefore important before you sign a rental or purchase contract. Contracts must be handled with great care and the assistance of an attorney, as they are long-term agreements and ignorance has cost many a business dearly. Read the fine print carefully. You can also negotiate an agreement that will be more beneficial for the business.

List the five most important factors that will play a role in the choice of a place of establishment for your own business. Also give reasons why you regard each of these considerations as important.

....

....

....

....

....

8 SETTING-UP FACTORS THAT ARE RELATED TO THE BUSINESS FUNCTIONS

The business functions were discussed briefly in Chapter 2. In this section we take a look at what must be done in respect of the business functions when a business is set up. The eight business functions are discussed separately, but there is a degree of overlap.

8.1 Initial marketing

As you saw in the example of the business plan in Chapter 5, it is important to plan the marketing of a business. Consider the target market, the variety of products and/or services that will be made available, at what price and how and where they will be made available (distribution). This is the core of the **marketing plan**.

TARGET MARKET		PRODUCT/SERVICES
	MARKETING	
DISTRIBUTION		PRICE

The marketing plan therefore provides answers to the following questions:

- ❏ Where are we now?
- ❏ Where do we want to be?
- ❏ How do we get there?
- ❏ How do we exercise control?

For the development of a detailed marketing plan, consult: Machado, R. 1996. *Marketing for a Small Business*. Cape Town: Juta.

Your business will need a **name**, an **emblem/logo** and a **motto**.

The name and possibly the motto of the business must be written or graphically designed in a striking way. The name of a business must not change for no reason, as there is marketing value in a name and related mottos and emblems. The name, motto and emblem must be chosen to be effective in the long term, as far as possible, and must not be tied to a period or fashion.

When setting up a business, you will also need to design and print **business cards**, **letterheads** and **contracts**. Note that the quality of the printing/stationery contributes to the image of the business. Plan the design and information provided on the stationery carefully to be cost-effective but striking.

- ❏ The name, motto and emblem of the business must be as descriptive as possible so that the prospective client knows at once what the business is offering: for example, Budget Car Rental.
- ❏ Provide as much information as possible on a business card about the services and/or product that the business offers. An informative business card is like a pamphlet, providing people with information they can keep for later use. So try to provide more than just the name, address and telephone number.

Compare prices for printing/stationery and do not have too much printing done in the setting-up stage. There are often changes that must be made for practical reasons that you are not always aware of at first.

Remember that the abbreviations cc or (Pty) Ltd and the registration number must always appear on stationery.

Find out what the best **form of communication** for your business is, where and how your competitors advertise, and in what other ways they market their products. Then consider the same advertising channels, but remember to distinguish your **advertisements** from those of competitors in a significant way. For the small business, **personal sales** are still one of the most important means of communication.

Also note the cost of advertisements and try to develop a method of monitoring the results of each advertisement. In this way you can determine their cost-effectiveness. An example is a person who gives quotations for garden services by appointment. When prospective clients call to make an appointment, find out how they heard of the business. Then the inquiries on each advert can be established. Of course, notice must also be taken of the cost and the number of sales per advert. Remember, however, that there are other factors that can affect the success rate of an advert. There may, for example, be certain days of the week on which consumers are in a better position to react. Evaluate advertising campaigns in the long term and do not expect miracles after the first or second placing of an advert.

8.2 External relations

Try as far as possible to make use of external relations to promote the **image** of your business. In external relations the image of the business as a whole is important. The goals of external relations include the creation of goodwill, mutual understanding, acceptance and cooperation with the interested parties of the business. It is often confused with marketing, which is responsible for promoting specific products or services.

Here are some hints on promoting external relations:
- ❏ Make use of acquaintances and friends who can make your business known; in other words, make use of the network of people and friends (in the process called 'networking');
- ❏ Invite journalists from the local newspaper to the opening of the business;   ☞

❏ Write an article yourself and send photographs with it for publication if someone from the press cannot be present;

❏ Ask for an article to be written about your business when you are placing advertisements in a publication.

It is important for you to use creative and even alternative methods of exposure to make your business known and to distinguish it from similar businesses.

An example of good external relations is a person who starts an exclusive coffee shop in his or her home and publicises it by sending personal invitations to the press, identified prospective clients and their friends and colleagues. The opening period lasted three days and those who were invited were entertained free of charge. The launch was personal, the refreshments and the service excellent and a foretaste of the quality of the coffee shop. After the introductory period many people were aware of the coffee shop, a strongly representative group of the target market visits it regularly and the owner can rely on personal recommendation.

It is also important to join relevant **organisations** and **associations**. Local chambers of commerce, business clubs, sports clubs – if, for example, you are selling sporting goods – the Master Builders' Association (for reference and protection in the building trade) are just a few examples of where valuable contacts can be built up.

8.9 Administration and record systems

From the first day a business starts trading, records must be kept of the information of the business. It is important to develop effective, user-friendly record-keeping and filing systems.

Some examples and requirements of record-keeping systems are:

❏ a system for keeping **information on clients** (client information) available;
❏ an **accounting system** that you understand and that is simple and effective;
❏ an effective **stock control system** is important if you have to carry stock;
❏ a system for the **control of cash**;
❏ a system for keeping records of **marketing, inquiries** and **sales**;
❏ records of **turnover and profit** for tax purposes and, among others, also for levies to local authorities.

Examples of aids to record-keeping are account books for book-keeping, filing cabinets, alphabetical and numeric files and card systems, diaries and computers.

The kind of information you must record will determine which filing system is the most effective. Clients for whom specifications and other documentation and information sheets must be kept will warrant a file for each client in a steel cabinet, arranged alphabetically. An example is a town and regional planner who opens a file for each client, and keeps plans and documents of the particular client and property in it. On the other hand, a card system will be sufficient for clients for whom only important details like names, addresses and personal information must be recorded. A hairdresser or beautician would use such a card system, for example. A computer can also be used in this case, but this is an expensive system if it is not also used for other purposes.

8.4 The financial function

Before starting a business, you must determine:

❏ **what** the capital requirement is to set up the business;
❏ **how** the capital requirement will be **financed**.

It is important that entrepreneurs use personal funds for a portion of the initial capital before approaching a bank for financing. Financing institutions generally require a certain amount of own investment, and therefore it is easier to obtain external funds if personal funds like savings, a package or an inheritance are available. This **ensures that entrepreneurs commit themselves** to the business. The assumption is that the entrepreneur will be better motivated to achieve success. Then, if the business fails, it will not only be the financial institution that will lose money but also the entrepreneur.

Ensure that you obtain the right finance for a specific business requirement. For a fixed asset, like a hotel with a large outstanding amount, you must obtain long-term financing. It would be unrealistic to finance a hotel by means of a short-term loan which must be repaid within five years. It is also not desirable to pay off equipment like a computer, which quickly becomes technologically outdated, over a long term.

Different financial institutions must be approached for **different requirements**. Financial institutions, such as Business Partners, the Industrial Development Corporation, the small and medium enterprise (SME) sections of banks and development corporations (e.g. KwaZulu Finance and Investment Corporation), can provide financing to address the needs of SMEs. Financing ranges from **direct loans** to **incentive schemes**, and programmes can be adapted to your specific requirements.

Khula, the wholesale finance division of the Department of Trade and Industry, makes finance available to small and medium enterprises through various retail financial intermediaries, including NGOs and banks. The aim of Khula's **credit guarantees** is to provide access to finance for SME owners who might not qualify for finance through normal banking channels. Khula financial schemes require lower collateral and a lower percentage of owner funds.

For more information on financing your enterprise and other related matters, such as incentive schemes, tender opportunities and new business opportunities, the website of the Business Referral and Information Network (BRAIN), at www.brain.org.za, covers everything of interest to the small business entrepreneur.

Develop a **basic accounting system**. It does not have to be complicated; but it must meet the needs of your business and you must be able to understand it.

Appoint an external book-keeper or accountant if you do not wish, or are not able to handle, the book-keeping yourself. The money that you pay for this service is worth it. For the small business it is sometimes possible to share an accountant with other businesses. Such a person will need to spend one or two days a week to do your business's accounts.

Draw up specific **cash budgets**. This is part of the planning for the next period. Adjust the budgets if necessary. Budgets are important, because they can give you an indication of when cash will be available and when cash-flow problems will be experienced. They are essential for planning and are also useful in the control of the activities of the business.

Maintain a **good relationship with your bank**. To obtain additional capital and to ensure a positive attitude on the part of the bank manager, it is important to meet your obligations punctually. If this is not possible for some reason or other, explain the situation to the bank manager so that alternative arrangements can be made. An informed bank manager contributes to a sound relationship.

Make provision for the **insurance** of stock, vehicles, contents of the office, contracts, equipment, buildings, etc.

If you sell on credit, make sure you check the **creditworthiness** of the client. Obtain information from the person so that trade references can be made. Information can be obtained at a price from credit bureaux. Determine beforehand on what terms credit will be granted, and stick to them.

Read financial magazines and **keep up with economic affairs** and developments in the business world, particularly economic factors like interest rates and inflation.

For more information on the financial management of a small business, consult Kritzinger, A.A.C. & Fourie, J.C.W. 1996. *Basic Principles of Financial Management for a Small Business*. Cape Town: Juta.

8.5 Staff

Staff planning and the appointment of the right staff are important. Note the following steps when you plan staff appointments:

❑ Draw up a list of all the tasks that must be performed in the business. ☞

- Group the tasks so that tasks that can be performed by a specific person can be combined. This combination of tasks is the **job description**.
- Determine what qualifications and skills the person must have to perform the tasks. These are the **job specifications** of the appointment.
- Then **recruit** the right persons. This can be done by:
  - placing advertisements and then conducting the interviews and inquiring about an applicant yourself;
  - using recruitment agencies, who then perform these functions (they charge a fee equal to 7–15% of an appointment's annual salary);
  - approaching training organisations like schools, technical colleges or tertiary institutions where teachers or lecturers can make recommendations;
  - signing a **contract** with the employee. In the contract, among other things, working hours, leave and sick leave specifications must be recorded;
  - Give a clear description of the post to the employee – preferably a **written job description**.

Appointing family or friends is often regarded as the ideal, but it has many pitfalls. Often an appointment is made because it is:

- the quickest or easiest method of appointment;
- to help a friend/family member;
- because the person has a specific characteristic that is clearly favourable for the business.

Doing this means that you do not compare the person with other suitable candidates for the post. Such an appointment must be done with great care, as it involves many complications of which you are initially not aware.

Examples of complications are:

- such a person does not have the necessary skills or qualifications;
- personal and working relationships differ;
- friction can arise, with adverse effects for the business;
- jealousy of the family member or friend towards you, the employer, due to personal involvement;

❑ family appointments and promotions can make other employees jealous;

❑ friction between other family members and friends.

6.6 The purchasing function

Find out about trade and speciality shows for specific industries. You can make purchases at shows, and obtain information about innovations and product developments in your area of business. You can also market your products at these shows. Examples are the SARDCA (South African Retailers, Dispensaries and Chemist Association), which is an annual show where wholesalers in gifts, household goods and interior decorations and general retail products display their products to retailers and service providers. Under one roof, buyers view a large variety of available products, and can place orders with various wholesalers. Similar shows are arranged for the catering, jewellery, construction, beauty, interior decorating, antique collectors, fashion industries, etc.

Negotiate with suppliers for better prices for cash, to obtain products on consignment or for 30-day accounts. The financial planning of the business will determine what is the most favourable method of payment for purchases.

Compare suppliers not only in terms of price, but also in terms of quality and the services they provide, such as delivery, installation, etc.

Purchases must be planned to **keep stock to a minimum** and to control it properly, as carrying stock costs money. The 'Just-in-Time' (JIT) system is an effective stock-control system that was originally developed in Japan. Stock is delivered just in time for use to limit the costs of carrying stock. However, it is essential to have sufficient stock on hand for sound client service.

Be careful **not to become too dependent on one supplier**. This can cause problems when this supplier is out of stock, prices become too high or service deteriorates. Find, and also make use of, alternative suppliers to ensure continuous good service. Obtain price lists, information on discounts and catalogues from various suppliers.

It is important to have **good relations with suppliers**. This ensures better service and is especially important in changing circumstances such as when there is a great demand for specific products and raw materials and the supplier has to decide which clients will be given preference.

8.7 Production

Production makes use of inputs like raw materials, products and services, which you as a business process to make your product or service (the outputs) possible. This applies only to manufacturing businesses and differs from business to business.

Manufacturing businesses must note the following:

❑ **The optimal use of equipment.** Meticulous planning in respect of machinery and other equipment is important so that you do not invest too much capital in it. At the same time, it is essential to make provision for sufficient equipment to ensure timely production.

❑ **Trained labour** to ensure correct use of equipment.

❑ **Expert design/knowledgeable layout** of production facilities.

❑ **Cost control** to ensure a profitable operation.

❑ **Built-in control measures** like inspections and operational procedures.

❑ **Production time**. Clients' orders must be executed as agreed and this requires careful planning of equipment and labour.

❑ **'Bottlenecks'** often occur when specialised labour and expensive equipment is involved. Sound planning is essential to avoid bottlenecks so that deliveries can be made on time.

❑ **Outsourcing** certain functions in the production process is an option, for example to:

   – eliminate specific bottlenecks. A building contractor will, for example, make use of subcontractors for carpentry in a certain contract when he/she is already making optimal use of the carpenters in his/her service.

   – postpone the purchase of expensive equipment. A business that manufactures doors and windows with aluminium frames will initially buy the door handles and window catches from a supplier. When sufficient profit has been made, it will purchase the equipment for making them.

☞

☞

> – ensure the availability of labour. A nursery will refer clients
> who are interested in a professionally designed garden to an
> independent, expert landscape architect. The nursery can offer
> this service to clients without being responsible for paying the
> person's salary. It can even make an agreement with the land-
> scape architect that he/she will buy all the plants and supplies
> from the nursery.

6.9 Management

The entrepreneur will be the manager of the business during its establishment stage. He or she is therefore responsible for:

- ❑ formulating **goals** for the business;
- ❑ **encouraging people** to achieve these goals;
- ❑ performing the **management functions**, namely planning, organisation, leadership and control.

Management involves the planning, organisation, leadership and control of
the various business functions and of the business as a unit. It also
involves the effective co-ordination of the business functions.

As few employees are usually appointed to management capacities in a
new business, the entrepreneur is responsible for the management of the
various business functions as well as the business as a whole. If there are
two or more directors or partners, each one is given specific business
functions to manage.

An outside person is sometimes appointed to perform a specific business
function, such as a marketing manager who is responsible for the entire
marketing function on a part-time basis. It is also possible to outsource
some functions. Consider the interior decorator who outsources the
production function. She/he does not manufacture the products for the
clients, but has it done by different contractors. The overall responsibility
for management, however, remains with the entrepreneur, who must
ensure that the business functions as a profitable whole.

When establishing a small business, it is essential to buy in or outsource
expertise which the entrepreneur lacks. This ensures cost-effectiveness and
makes effective management possible.

It is also management's responsibility to determine the optimal operating capacity of the business. A business reaches its optimal operating capacity when inputs, labour and/or production factors are used to the maximum to ensure the maximum output. When a new business is established, it seldom functions optimally from the start. There are therefore usually fewer orders or a lesser demand than can be provided. The entrepreneur possibly starts below or at the break-even point, with the prospect of obtaining more business so that he or she can in time function optimally. This will ensure increased profits. Remember, however, that the availability of specific equipment and labour is crucial to the production of a particular quantity of products.

If the demand exceeds the determined maximum output, additional costs must be incurred to meet this demand. Often it is not possible to make provision only for the particular increase in demand. Suppose the demand for a product rises by 100 units. The equipment for manufacturing the 100 additional products costs R12 000. This expenditure, however, causes the production capacity to be raised and an additional 800 products can be manufactured. Then a new break-even point must be calculated to determine for what increased demand it is worth raising the production capacity. If the demand does not justify the purchase of additional equipment, other methods must be found to increase outputs. Examples are:

❑ overtime;
❑ producing in quiet periods for stock build-up;
❑ contracting out certain functions or processes;
❑ contracting out for the manufacture of specific quantities of products;
❑ hiring equipment;
❑ appointing temporary labour and/or labour on contract.

Thus the entrepreneur must ensure that the possible expansion of the business results in a real increase in income. The expense must not exceed the expected income as a result of the expansion of capacity. In certain cases, like when a constant increase in demand is expected, higher expenses than income are acceptable at first. In such a case, it is important that meaningful forecasts and planning takes place to ensure profitability, in the long term if not in the short term.

An important responsibility of the management is to draw up well-considered contracts between relevant parties. These include contracts between the business and:

- ❑ employees;
- ❑ landlords;
- ❑ clients.

Clear and unambiguous contracts avoid financial and personal and even legal conflicts.

The increase in the number of women entering the labour market, and the demanding nature of their occupations, causes them to have less time for domestic duties. A need arises to contract out certain domestic duties, hence for example the increasing popularity of restaurants, take-away meals and convenience stores like Spar and home industries. An entrepreneur, Riedwaan Jacobs, realises that he can provide a service to career women, among others. He starts a grocery delivery service. Groceries, fresh products, meat and liquor are delivered to the clients on order once a week. By making use of his service, a client saves valuable time, which is then available for families, careers and interests that demand personal involvement.

Briefly discuss what Riedwaan must do in respect of each business function when he sets up the new business. (Use a separate piece of paper.)

SUMMARY

When a new business is established, the setting-up and establishment factors are not equal for all businesses. The entrepreneur has to determine which factors are critical for the success of the proposed business. In planning the business he or she must concentrate on these factors. Remember that the emphasis of the business often shifts and that growth makes different demands on the entrepreneur. A business that at first had few or no staff will have to appoint more staff eventually, or an entrepreneur who does his or her own marketing at first will later make use of a marketing specialist. The entrepreneur must therefore note the **critical success factors** in the setting-up stage, but be aware of the fact that the situation is not static. Change comes rapidly in business and it is important to make provision for it in time to ensure competitiveness.

10 SELF-EVALUATION

1. List the most suitable form of business for the business that you are planning and give three reasons for your choice.

   ....

   ....

   ....

   ....

2. Which legal registrations and requirements for licensing are applicable to the business you wish to establish?

   ....

   ....

   ....

   ....

   ....

3. List the most important factors in the choice of a site for the business that you are planning and indicate why each plays a rôle.

   ....

   ....

   ....

   ....

   ....

4. To which operational elements of the business functions must attention be given in the setting-up stage of your proposed business? How will you manage each business function in the setting-up stage? Each business function must be discussed on a separate sheet of paper.

]] ADDENDUM 1

CONTRACT OF EMPLOYMENT (Indefinite Period)

It is hereby agreed that a contract for an indefinite period be entered into between

....

(who shall be referred to hereinafter as THE EMPLOYER) – and

....

Identity No ....

(who shall be referred to hereinafter as THE EMPLOYEE).

NOW THEREFORE THE PARTIES HAVE AGREED TO THE FOLLOWING TERMS AND CONDITIONS

1. JOB TITLE
The EMPLOYEE shall be employed as ....

....

2. STARTING DATE
The EMPLOYEE shall commence his/her employment on: .... for an indefinite period.

3. DUTIES
The EMPLOYEE shall be expected to satisfactorily carry out all the tasks and duties normally associated with the position. The EMPLOYEE agrees and undertakes to obey all reasonable and lawful orders and instructions which may be given by any person employed by The EMPLOYER who is in a managerial or supervisory position. The EMPLOYEE confirms that he/she is capable and competent to perform the duties for which he/she has been employed, and that he/she has the necessary skills and knowledge to perform competently and to the satisfaction of The EMPLOYER. It is expressly agreed by the EMPLOYEE that should the work, as set out in the job description, be unavailable he/she will be prepared to perform any other suitable work which falls within his/her vocational abilities provided that it shall be without loss of remuneration. The performance of any other suitable work under these circumstances will not be seen as a right of the EMPLOYEE and

the EMPLOYER reserves the right to retrench the EMPLOYEE in these circumstances. Further details: ....

....

4. EVALUATION OF PERFORMANCE
The EMPLOYEE'S performance, skill, conduct, compatibility, knowledge and health will be evaluated by the EMPLOYER, and any failure by the EMPLOYEE to comply or meet with the above conditions or standards may lead to a disciplinary investigation and appropriate disciplinary steps.

5. REMUNERATION
5.1 The EMPLOYEE'S basic salary / wage shall be R.............................per month/week and payment shall be made monthly/weekly in arrears not later than the last day of each month.

5.2 Payment of the EMPLOYEE'S salary/wage shall be made either by cheque or be paid into the EMPLOYEE'S account at a financial institution of his/her choice.

5.3 Salary raise will be contemplated on grounds of merit or otherwise once per year.

5.4 Bonus paid shall be at the EMPLOYER'S own discretion and dependent on the company's financial situation.
 – After 12 months
 – Any bonuses paid will be paid in December of each year.
 – Any bonus which may be paid to the EMPLOYEE will be determined on merit or at an amount of R.................................

- If the EMPLOYEE terminates services before completion of 12 months of service, no bonus will be payable.

5.5 In terms of days or time absent from work without permission or leave, no money will be paid to the EMPLOYEE and such absent time will be deducted from any bonus payable.

5.6 Overtime is payable by 1,5 of normal wages.

5.7 Service rendered on a Sunday or public holiday will be paid at a rate of double time.

5.8 Meals and rations. The EMPLOYER will provide: Breakfast ....
Lunch ....
Supper ....
on working days as determine by EMPLOYER from time to time. Meals and rations will be considered as having the value of R............... per month.

5.9 Transport allowance of R......................... per week/month will be paid for transport to and from work.

5.10 Payment in kind:
Accommodation – Value R.........................
Food – Value R...

5.11 Deductions: The following deductions will be made from the EMPLOYEE'S remuneration:
Medical Fund: ....
PAYE:..
Pension Fund:..
UIF: ....
Other:...
W.C.:...

5.12 INCREASES
Future increases will be based on the EMPLOYEE'S individual performance as well as on the overall financial performance of the EMPLOYER'S undertaking during the preceding financial year. Such granting of increases (when applicable) will be entirely at the discretion of the EMPLOYER and will take place during .... of each year. The EMPLOYEE agrees that any increases granted in terms of this clause will be set off against any wage increase which may become due and payable according to any wage regulating measure or other agreement if such increase takes effect within 11 months of the granting of the aforesaid increase.

5.13 ANNUAL BONUS
The EMPLOYER shall pay to the EMPLOYEE an annual bonus at the end of each calendar year, subject to the EMPLOYEE being in the employ of the EMPLOYER at that time, depending on the performance of the EMPLOYEE and the EMPLOYER'S financial standing. If the EMPLOYEE had not completed a full year of employment with the EMPLOYER, then the bonus shall be calculated on a pro rata basis according to the period that the EMPLOYEE had worked. No bonus shall be paid if the EMPLOYEE'S employment is terminated prior to the end of the calendar year. All bonuses will be paid at the EMPLOYER'S discretion.

6. ANNUAL LEAVE

6.1 The EMPLOYEE will be entitled to .... continuous days of paid vacation leave at the end of each year of employment. Such leave shall be taken in accordance with the prescribed leave rules and regulations and at a time agreed to by the EMPLOYER at its discretion. The EMPLOYEE agrees to take such leave during the annual shutdown period.

Alternatively, one day's leave for every 17 days worked will be calculated.

6.2 For every public holiday during the leave of the EMPLOYEE, which would have otherwise been a normal working day for him/her, an extra day's leave will be added.

6.3 A regular day EMPLOYEE will be entitled to 1 day's leave for every 17 days worked.

7. SICK LEAVE

7.1 An EMPLOYEE is entitled to paid sick leave equal to the number of days the EMPLOYEE would normally work during a period of 6 weeks during every cycle of 36 months worked. Sick leave not taken will not be paid out. If more than 2 continuous days' sick leave is taken, the EMPLOYEE must submit an acceptable doctor's certificate. If continual illness occurs, the EMPLOYER may insist on a doctor's certificate for every day off. If the EMPLOYER does not accept the EMPLOYEE'S explanation the EMPLOYER will assist the EMPLOYEE to undergo a medical examination.

During the first six months of employment, the EMPLOYEE will be entitled to 1 day's paid sick leave for every 26 days worked.

7.2 If the EMPLOYEE is absent for an unreasonably long time, due to illness, the employer is entitled to terminate the contract after a procedurally fair investigation into the health position of the EMPLOYEE.

7.3 The EMPLOYEE guarantees that at the time of signing the agreement, he/she is free of any terminal or contagious illness.

7.4 If the EMPLOYEE should discover any such illness after employment, he/she will immediately inform the EMPLOYER.

7.5 The EMPLOYEE agrees to a medical examination requested by the EMPLOYER, at any reasonable time, with the EMPLOYER bearing the cost and access to all medical reports.

7.6 The EMPLOYEE hereby authorises the EMPLOYER to deduct medical costs of the EMPLOYEE from the EMPLOYEE'S salary.

8. MATERNITY LEAVE (Unpaid leave)

8.1 Maternity leave will commence at any time from four weeks before the expected date of birth, unless otherwise agreed or when a medical practitioner or midwife certifies that it is necessary for the EMPLOYEE'S health or that of her unborn child. (S.25(2)b).

8.2 A female EMPLOYEE must commence maternity leave from 4 weeks before the expected birth until 6 weeks after the birth unless a medical practitioner or midwife certifies that she is fit to work. The EMPLOYEE is entitled to at least 4 consecutive months' maternity leave.

8.3 The EMPLOYEE will notify an EMPLOYER in writing, unless the EMPLOYEE is unable to do so, of the date on which she intends to commence with maternity leave and return to work at least 4 weeks before such date, unless the EMPLOYEE is unable to do so. (A.25 & 26)

8.4 The EMPLOYEE understands that she will be considered as having deserted if she does not report for duty within five days after the stipulated date. A disciplinary investigation will be held regarding the reasons for the absence.

9. FAMILY RESPONSIBILITY LEAVE

Where the EMPLOYEE has completed 4 months' service and works for at least 4 days a week, the EMPLOYEE will be entitled to 3 days of paid leave per leave cycle:

1) when the EMPLOYEE'S child is born;
2) when the EMPLOYEE'S child is sick; or
3) in the event of the death of:
   (i) the EMPLOYEE'S spouse or life partner; ....
   or
   (ii) the EMPLOYEE'S parent, adoptive parent, grandparent, child, adopted child, grandchild or sibling. (S.27)

10. PUBLIC HOLIDAYS

The following public holidays will be paid and will be exchangeable for any other day. New Year's Day, Human Rights Day, Good Friday, Family Day, Freedom Day, EMPLOYEES' Day, Youth Day, National Women's Day, Heritage Day, Day of Reconciliation, Christmas Day, Day of Goodwill. When one of the public holidays falls on a Sunday, the following Monday shall be a public holiday. The EMPLOYEE agrees that any public holiday shall be exchangeable for any other day which the EMPLOYER chooses. The EMPLOYEE will not be entitled to public holidays during strikes.

The EMPLOYEE agrees to work on any public holiday should this be required by the EMPLOYER.

11. TERMINATION OF EMPLOYMENT

The EMPLOYEE'S service may be terminated by either him/her or by the EMPLOYER by giving not less than 1 week's written notice during the first 4 weeks of employment. After four weeks, but during the first year, 2 weeks' notice will be given and 4 weeks if the EMPLOYEE has 1 year's service and more. Either party may summarily terminate this Contract for any cause recognised by law as being sufficient, subject to this being reduced to writing. This agreement may be terminated by the EMPLOYER without any notice or any payment in lieu of notice in the case of gross misconduct or dishonesty on the part of the

EMPLOYEE. The EMPLOYER will in such event follow the procedure laid down in the disciplinary code and procedure.

12. HOURS OF WORK

12.1 The EMPLOYEE'S ordinary hours of work shall be .... hours per day, and shall be from .... to .... on Mondays to Thursdays and from ....to.............on Fridays, and from ....to............ on Saturdays.

The EMPLOYEE will be entitled to the following breaks during any one day:

(i) ....

(ii) ....

(iii) ....

The EMPLOYEE agrees to a 30-minute lunch break.

The total weekly working hours will be the following: ....

12.2 OVERTIME

Overtime is a condition of employment and the EMPLOYEE undertakes to work the statutory prescribed maximum overtime, currently 3 hours per day and 10 hours per week, provided that:

- the EMPLOYER notifies the EMPLOYEE during the preceding day that he/she is required to work overtime; and
- nothing in this Agreement shall limit the EMPLOYER'S right and the EMPLOYEE'S obligation to work emergency overtime on short notice.
- Overtime payment will be made in terms of the applicable conditions of employment at a rate of 1,5 times the basic daily rate on the normal pay day.

13. DESERTION AS BREACH OF CONTRACT

The EMPLOYEE agrees that should he/she fail to report for work for more than 5 consecutive days without notifying the EMPLOYER and providing the EMPLOYER with satisfactory proof, it will constitute serious breach of contract and he/she shall be deemed to have deserted.

14. CONFIDENTIALITY

The EMPLOYEE shall not divulge any information to any unauthorised persons or bodies relating to any aspect of his/her work or to any of the operations or processes of the EMPLOYER. Such information shall include methods, processes, computer software, documentation, client lists, programmes, trade secrets, technical information, chemical formulae, drawings, financial information or any other information which could be damaging to the EMPLOYER'S operations or which could benefit other parties to the detriment of the EMPLOYER. Such restrictions shall apply during and after the EMPLOYEE'S employment with the EMPLOYER.

15. RULES AND REGULATIONS

The EMPLOYEE will observe and obey all the rules, regulations and procedures which have been or may be drawn up by the EMPLOYER, or where applicable, the Bargaining Council or any relevant legislation. The EMPLOYER will endeavour to ensure that the EMPLOYEE is made familiar with such rules, regulations and procedures. The EMPLOYER reserves the right to change or add any of its rules, regulations and procedures at any time at its discretion, subject to reasonable notice to the EMPLOYEE. The EMPLOYEE confirms that he/she has been given a copy of the disciplinary code with this contract and that it has been explained to him/her.

16. INDUSTRIAL ACTION

The EMPLOYEE agrees not to take part in or to incite any other person to participate in any illegal industrial action which may adversely affect any of the EMPLOYER'S operations. Such action may include, but is not limited to strikes, go-slows, work to rule, boycotts, stayaways or any other similar action which may obstruct, prevent or retard the work of other EMPLOYEES or the EMPLOYER'S operations. The EMPLOYEE agrees to participate only in legal industrial action which may have arisen after the statutory dispute-settling procedures having been followed. The EMPLOYEE agrees to assist the EMPLOYER in endeavouring to promote, enhance and maintain industrial peace and harmony in the workplace. This agreement will automatically be suspended during a strike.

17. PLACE OF EMPLOYMENT

The place of employment will be:

....
....
....

It will also be required that EMPLOYEE work at the following places:

....
....
....

18. RELEVANT PREVIOUS SERVICE

Period of previous employment that is relevant for this contract.

....
....

19. LIST OF RELEVANT DOCUMENTATION (NOT INCLUDED IN THIS DOCUMENT)

Will be available at the company's offices where a copy may be obtained.

....
....
....

20. HEALTH

The EMPLOYEE confirms that he/she is in good physical and mental health and is capable of carrying out all the duties assigned to him/her by the EMPLOYER. Should the EMPLOYEE be found not to be able to perform his/her duties in a competent and proper manner to the satisfaction of the EMPLOYER, due to health reasons, then the EMPLOYER shall reserve the right to terminate the EMPLOYEE'S services. The EMPLOYER may require the EMPLOYEE to undergo any medical examination at the expense of the EMPLOYER from time to time in order to ascertain the state of the EMPLOYEE'S health. The EMPLOYEE certifies that he/she has not contracted or does not suffer from any serious contagious disease such as AIDS, hepatitis B, meningitis, leprosy, etc. Should

the EMPLOYEE contract any such serious contagious disease, then he/she shall inform the EMPLOYER immediately, who will have the right to decide whether to terminate the EMPLOYEE'S employment.

The EMPLOYER is herewith authorised to inform any person whose health could be affected by this situation.

21. WORK OUTSIDE EMPLOYMENT

The EMPLOYEE shall not be entitled to work, outside normal working hours, for any other employer, or conduct his/her own business, unless the nature of his/her involvement has been revealed to the EMPLOYER and the written consent of the EMPLOYER has been obtained. A further condition is that the undertaking of the other PARTY'S business shall not, directly or indirectly, be in competition with the undertaking of the EMPLOYER and the EMPLOYEE'S involvement may not in any way whatsoever detrimentally affect the EMPLOYEE'S work or his/her working relationship with the EMPLOYER.

22. SAFETY AND SECURITY

22.1 The EMPLOYEE agrees to observe and obey all the safety and security rules and regulations as prescribed by the EMPLOYER, and/or the Occupational Safety and Health Act.

22.2 The EMPLOYEE declares that he/she has never been convicted of a Schedule 1 criminal offence as contained in the Criminal Procedure Act 51 of 1977, such offences being theft, fraud, assault, rape, arson, etc. The EMPLOYEE agrees that should this statement be proved to be false, or should the EMPLOYEE fail to declare a future Schedule 1 offence, the EMPLOYER will reserve the right to summarily terminate the EMPLOYEE'S service.

22.3 The EMPLOYEE agrees that the EMPLOYER or persons appointed by him may, from time to time, conduct searches of the EMPLOYEE'S person or personal possessions for security or safety reasons. Such searches may include any vehicle of the EMPLOYEE which may enter the premises of the EMPLOYER.

22.4 The EMPLOYEE shall wear any security identity card which the EMPLOYER may issue, at all times on entering, leaving or being on the premises of the EMPLOYER.

23. PATENTS AND COPYRIGHT

23.1 The EMPLOYER shall reserve the right to retain all and/or any rights to any patents or copyright to any inventions, designs, discoveries, improvements as made, discovered or conceived by the EMPLOYEE during his/her employment with the EMPLOYER whether wholly or partly, and whether in connection with or incidental to his/her employment with the EMPLOYER, and which may relate to, or be in connection with, or be useful to the business carried out by the EMPLOYER whether or not during normal working hours and whether or not at the EMPLOYER'S premises. Such patents or copyrights shall not be limited to any particular area or country and the EMPLOYER shall have the right to alter, modify, adapt or change any designs, processes or methods of any such patents or copyrights.

23.2 The EMPLOYEE shall not copy, print or publish any of the EMPLOYER'S methods, processes, procedures relating to the business of the EMPLOYER unless permission has been granted by the EMPLOYER to do so.

23.3 Should, within 1 year after the termination of his/her employment with the EMPLOYER, the EMPLOYEE either alone or jointly with another person or body originate, invent or design any Industrial Property in relation to any product or process upon which he/she worked or which came to his/her attention during the last 2 years of his/her employment with the EMPLOYER or for which copyright had been obtained, such as Industrial Property, the EMPLOYEE'S interest therein shall automatically vest in the EMPLOYER.

23.4 The EMPLOYEE hereby binds him/herself and undertakes that he/she shall:
- immediately communicate full details of such Industrial Property to the EMPLOYER and to no other person;
- without expense to the EMPLOYEE sign all such documents and do all such acts as

may be required by the EMPLOYER in order to vest formal title in such Industrial Property in the EMPLOYER and/or to enable the EMPLOYER to apply for local or foreign patents, registered designs or trade marks in respect thereof;
- in those countries in which a patent or design application may only be filed in the name of the inventor or author, he/she will at the request of the EMPLOYER, but at the latter's expense, sign the documents as may be required by the EMPLOYER to enable a patent or design application to be filed therein in respect of such Industrial Property and subsequently to assign the same to the EMPLOYER.

24. TRAINING

The EMPLOYER may require the EMPLOYEE to attend, from time to time, training courses or development programmes in order to improve the EMPLOYEE'S skills, knowledge or experience. Attendance at these courses or programmes will be at the discretion and expense of the EMPLOYER.

25. DEDUCTIONS

The EMPLOYEE authorises the EMPLOYER to deduct from his/her earnings, any monies owing to the EMPLOYER for whatever reason, irrespective whether the EMPLOYEE is in the employ of the EMPLOYER at the time of such deductions.

26. CHANGE OF STATUS

The EMPLOYEE shall, within a reasonable period, notify the EMPLOYER of any change in his/her status, such as address, dependants, marital, telephone number, qualifications or any other relevant changes.

27. DATE OF RETIREMENT

The EMPLOYEE will retire at the age of ....55/60/65 or as otherwise agreed in writing.

28. ADDRESS DOMICILIA

Should either party serve any notice on the other, this shall be done in writing, which may be delivered by hand or sent by registered post to the address hereunder and such address will be accepted as the address (*domicilium citandi et executandi*) for all legal intents and purposes concerning this Contract.

For the EMPLOYEE: ....

For the EMPLOYER : ....

29. PLACE OF EMPLOYMENT

29.1 The place of employment will be (address):

....

....

....

29.2 TRANSFER

Should the need arise, the EMPLOYER retains the right to transfer the EMPLOYEE to any other business of the EMPLOYER in any position on a temporary or permanent basis, after consultation and reasonable notice to the EMPLOYEE. Refusal by the EMPLOYEE to such a transfer, without an acceptable or lawful reason, will amount to breach of contract.

30. OFFENCES

The EMPLOYEE undertakes immediately to notify the EMPLOYER in the event of the endorsement of his driver's licence or any criminal offence with regard to dishonesty or violence.

31. IN GENERAL

31.1 This Contract shall be the entire agreement between the parties and no variation, alteration and/or addition will be of any force or effect unless placed in writing and signed by both parties.

31.2 No indulgence, leniency or extension of time which the parties may grant each other, in the event of claims and/or disputes shall in any way whatsoever prejudice either of them, preclude either of them from exercising their rights or constitute a waiver or limitation of any of their respective rights.

31.3 Both parties acknowledge that by signing this Contract, they have received a copy of this Contract, and they have read and understood the contents thereof. Both parties undertake to hold themselves bound by this Contract and agree to observe the provisions contained therein.

31.4 GUARANTEE BY EMPLOYEE

The EMPLOYEE confirms that all documentation, information and credentials presented to the EMPLOYER in support of his/her application for employment are authentic and it is agreed that in the event of any of the above subsequently proving to be false, this will be grounds for summary termination of the EMPLOYEE'S services.

31.5 ACCESS

The EMPLOYEE agrees that any legal right he/she has to be on the EMPLOYER'S premises is dependent upon the adequate performance of the duties allocated to him/her by the EMPLOYER. It is therefore specifically agreed that should the EMPLOYEE, for whatever reason, decide not to proceed with the performance of his/her allocated duties he/she shall at the request of the EMPLOYER leave the EMPLOYER'S premises in an orderly manner within 20 (twenty) minutes after being requested to do so and that refusal or failure to do so will be regarded as breach of contract.

31.6 The parties agree that all the terms and conditions of employment are:

– specified in this agreement and

– those conditions of employment not specified in this agreement shall be in terms of the EMPLOYER'S rules, regulations and procedures and the Bargaining Council agreement for the .... Industry, and

– that in the event that this Employment Contract, the Bargaining Council agreement and the EMPLOYER'S rules, regulations and procedures are silent on any specific point then, the relevant section(s) of the Basic Conditions of Employment Act 75 of 1997 (as amended) shall apply.

Signed at .... on this .... day of .... 20 ....

EMPLOYEE:...
I understand the conditions of the contract as explained and interpreted to me and accept it voluntarily.

I do not need an interpreter:...

INTERPRETER: ....

NAME: ....

SIGNATURE: ....
The conditions were explained and interpreted for the EMPLOYEE and are voluntarily accepted by the EMPLOYEE.

WITNESSES:

1 ....

2 ....

EMPLOYER: ....

WITNESSES:

1 ....

2 ....

11 REFERENCES

Amos, T. & Ristow, A. 1999. *Human Resource Management*. Cape Town: Juta.

Cilliers, H.S., Benade, M.L., Henning, J.J., Du Plessis, J.J., Delport, P.A., Fourie, J.S.A., De Koker, L. & Pretorius, J.T. 2000. *Entrepreneurial Law*. 2nd edition. Durban: Butterworth.

Department of Labour. 1995. Labour Relations Act 66 of 1995. *Government Gazette*, vol. 366, no. 16861. Cape Town. 13 December 1995. http://www.polity.org/govdocs/legislation/1995/act95-066.html.

Department of Labour. 1997. Basic Conditions of Employment Act 75 of 1997. http://www.polity.org/govdocs/regulations/1998/reg98-1438.html.

Department of Labour. 1998. Employment Equity Act 55 of 1998. *Government Gazette*, vol. 400, no. 1323. Cape Town. 19 October 1998.

Jones, G. 1988. *Starting Up*. 2nd edition. London: Pitman Publishing.

Le Roux, E.E., Venter, C.H., Jansen van Vuuren, J.E., Jacobs, H., Labuschagne, M., Kritzinger, A.A., Ferreira, E.J., de Beer, A.A. & Hubner, C.P. 1995. *Ondernemingsbestuur: 'n Praktiese benadering*. Johannesburg: Lexicon Uitgewers.

Levinson, J.C. 1984. *Guerilla Marketing: Secrets for Making Big Profits from Your Small Business*. Boston: Houghton Mifflin Company.

Van der Walt, H. (ed.) 1999. *Code for Fair Labour Practice*. Florida Hills: P&R de Bod.